Look Up and Dream

ROBERT RIETTI

Foreword by
Chief Rabbi Professor Jonathan Sacks

VALLENTINE MITCHELL
LONDON • PORTLAND, OR

First published in 1999 by Vallentine Mitchell

Middlesex House,
29/45 High Street, Edgware,
Middlesex HA8 7UU, UK

920 NE 58th Avenue, Suite 300
Portland, Oregon,
97213-3786 USA

www.vmbooks.com

British Library Cataloguing in Publication Data

Rietti, Robert.
Look Up and Dream.
1. Curiosities and Wonders. 2. Fate and Fatalism.
3. Miracles.
I. Title
001.9'4

ISBN 978 0 85303 353 0 (paper)

Library of Congress Cataloging-in-Publication Data
An entry can be found on request

Printed by Good News Digital Books, Stevenage, Hertfordshire

For Tina

'As the years go by, I realize more and more that
– no matter what is my problem –
you are the answer

Contents

Part III – His Mysterious Ways

Part IV – Of People and Things

Foreword

PETER BERGER, the eminent sociologist, calls them 'signals of transcendence' – moments when the veil of chance that covers human affairs is lifted and we catch a glimpse of something vast beyond.

The Bible describes one such episode. Joseph, Jacob's beloved son, has been sent by his father to visit his brothers who are tending the flocks some distance away. We, the readers, know that this will be a fateful encounter. Joseph's dreams have upset the brothers. So too has the favoured treatment he has received from his father. His siblings are jealous. They can no longer 'speak peaceably' with Joseph. What will happen when they meet far away from home? From all the clues supplied thus far, we know that this will be more than a routine occasion. Something will happen that will have consequences for the rest of their lives.

Yet it is at just this point of unfolding drama that the whole story seems to be about to end in anti-climax. Joseph arrives at his destination but the brothers are nowhere to be seen. Someone – a man whose name we never learn – comes across him 'wandering around in the fields', lost and looking for something or someone. The Bible describes the conversation that ensues. 'What are you looking for?' asks the stranger. 'My brothers', Joseph replies. 'They've moved on', says the man. 'I heard them say, "Let's go to Dothan"'. Joseph goes off in that direction and eventually sees the brothers in the distance. It's a curious episode. The Bible rarely, if ever, describes such inconsequential matters. The question we are bound to ask is not, Did it happen? but rather, Why does it form part of the story?

The answer supplied by traditional commentary is that the unnamed man who found Joseph and set him on his way was an angel, meaning an emissary of God. Yet even this is a curious answer, in need of further explanation. Angels in the Bible usually have a determinate mission, a message to deliver. Joseph's stranger gives him no such message. He merely supplies him with information as might any passer-by.

But the tradition was surely right. Everything about the story of Joseph suggests that we are engaged in a drama whose theme is the intervention of Divine providence in the affairs of mankind. Nothing is what it appears on the surface. The way is being prepared for the fulfilment of the vision granted Abraham long before: that eventually his descendants would suffer exile in a strange land as a prelude to their emergence as a people. Joseph and his brothers, unbeknown to them, are characters whose script has been written and whose development is being directed by an altogether supernatural hand. And, as if to remind us of the fact, every so often something happens to move them back on course. In the context of the drama, the meeting between Joseph and the stranger is something other than a chance encounter. It too is part of the script. The stranger has been placed there by Heaven. He himself may not know it, but he has a part to play in the predestined course of events. The thirteenth-century commentator Nahmanides put it best when he wrote that the man was 'an angel who did not know he was an angel'.

What a delightful phrase! And here, perhaps, lies the clue to the sense we sometimes have, as we look back on the apparently random events that have happened to us and see that they played a vital part in the narrative of our life. Were they mere chance? Or were they perhaps something more: the gentle touch of Providence setting us back on the path from which we had wandered? Were the people we met, whose names we may never have discovered, themselves 'angels who did not know they were angels'? So, at any rate, it may seem to those for whom human affairs are conducted under the watchful eye of Heaven. What looks now like chance may, in retrospect, come more and more to seem like fateful intervention, the Divine hand moving the pieces of the human checkerboard – in short, a 'signal of transcendence'.

That is the recurring theme of Robert Rietti's engaging reminiscences, *Look Up and Dream*. Time and again he tells us of occasions in which the hand of God seems to have been directing the affairs of man. He calls them 'small miracles'. Coincidence? Happenstance? Luck? So they might seem to one for whom that is all there is, for whom the universe circles endlessly in the void, blind to our hopes, deaf to our prayers. But Rietti speaks to us with the voice of faith, real faith, not the hectoring variety convinced of its own righteousness, all too ready to use the perfection of God as a rod to chastise the imperfections of mankind. His, rather, is the faith of one who stands always open to surprise, his ear carefully attuned to the music of God beneath the noise and clamour of daily events. Rietti knows what we too often forget: that God speaks to us in the 'still, small voice', meaning the voice that we only hear if we are listening. To one without faith, life all too often confirms his or her lack of expectations. But to one for whom the presence of God is a perpetual possibility, Heaven discloses itself, often when we are least expecting it.

'Trust in the providence of God', Hubert van Zeller reminds us, 'is not a heaven-sent formula for the indolent, not a way of bypassing responsibility with regard to social and material concerns'. Instead, 'you have to take on the affairs that come your way, knowing that they come from God and must be steered back again to him'. What emerges from Rietti's stories is just this sense of wonder that, in the midst of everyday life, there can suddenly shine the brilliance of the

Divine light, reminding us that we are not alone, microorganisms on the surface of infinity. There is Someone who watches and hears, guiding our way, answering our prayers. Sometimes all we need to do is stop and listen, and we too will hear.

This is a lovely and moving book, inviting us to look at our lives again and recognise the moments at which we were touched by the sheltering wings of Divine providence and for a moment felt the whisper of eternity, signalling a purpose beyond the winds of chance and a Presence behind the rush of everyday events.

JONATHAN SACKS
Chief Rabbi, The United Hebrew
Congregations of the Commonwealth
London, November 1998

Introduction

I T ALL BEGAN in New York. I had been asked by Donald Rugoff who ran 'Cinema V' to dub one trial reel of a beautiful French film called *The Two of Us,* and to take the reel personally to show to him. If he were satisfied, a contract would follow to complete the film.

I arrived in New York and declared the contents of the film can to the customs officer, only to have it taken from me with the remark, 'We'll need to examine it first, to be sure there's no pornographic material there. You'll get it back in about four days.' Four days! At that time we were allowed to take only a few pounds out of England, and I was expecting to stay only one night in New York. How was I going to survive for four?

Rugoff was very generous and had booked me a comfortable room at the Drake Hotel in Manhattan, where he left me a message to say, 'You must be tired – rest today and come to see me tomorrow.' I hadn't the courage to tell him I had so little money to last out four days while we waited for customs to clear the reel, so I confined myself to eating only an evening meal in the hotel itself, and passed the daytime strolling through the streets of New York. I never realized before how enjoyable walking could be, and it enabled me to 'discover' the city in a way I might otherwise never have done. Most of my foreign trips had been for work, usually tightly sandwiched between London engagements, and more often than not on arriving I'd be whisked away to an underground studio to work like a demon, and leave the city just in time to catch the plane back, without ever having had the luxury of sightseeing or relaxing.

Walking the city brought rich dividends for I discovered a bookshop in a side-street far from the centre, where – among the 'publishers' remainders' – I found a book on prayer for one dollar. That book inspired me to create a programme entitled *The Language of Prayer* which I offered to Revd Kennedy Bell ('K.B.' as he was known to everyone at the BBC). He was then in charge of the early morning *Prayer for the Day* programme. K.B. was an upstanding, delightful, honest and wonderful man who became a true friend. For him I prepared a great many talks on the 'language of prayer' – and later I embarked on a series of true stories which my 'antennae' had picked up from friends, acquaintances and relatives, and which most people would label mere coincidence, but to me (and, dare I hope, not only to me) there is recognizably something more than that. Shall we call it 'His Hand'?

To my surprise and delight, these talks proved highly successful and led to further contributions for Roy Trevivian, Crispin Hollis and others in the Religious Department of the BBC and more recently to television programmes for Revd Dr Nelson Gray on Scottish Television.

The following is a selection of these talks, plus others I have written for broadcasting. The talks amount to several hundreds in all, and have prompted a response of at least as many letters from much treasured listeners, one of whom wrote to me not long ago to request a copy of one particular talk. Unfortunately I did not appear to have kept it, so I suggested that if she would take the trouble to write and ask 'Auntie' BBC, I was sure 'she' would oblige. My correspondent later sent me the reply she received which stated: 'After extensive research, I have to inform you that no one in this department has ever heard of Robert Rietti.' Perhaps that should be my epitaph?

Part I

His Hand

Rachel's Roubles

WHO HAS NOT been close to death at least once in his span and later tossed off his escape with the old war-time expression, 'Oh well, my number wasn't up yet'?

That extremely casual approach gives one food for thought. If, after all, one was destined not to die just then, how did one escape? In these days of television super-heroes, miraculous evasion is taken for granted, but, as few of us are gifted with the resourcefulness of '007', in that split second before the scales dropped, presumably something other than our own ingenuity tipped them in our favour. It is then that the thought occurs, 'Could He have been there?'

Take the event of the roubles. My mother was one of five children born to Russian parents living in Brestlitovsk during the Czar's regime. Her father, Maurice Rosenay, owned a large furniture store which was frequented by the well-to-do army officers stationed in that military town. Maurice was financially secure enough to offer a good home to his wife and children – but, of course, schooling was a problem for Jewish families. Children were seldom permitted to attend State schools, movement between one city and another was severely restricted, and every religious holiday became the cue for a 'pogrom'.

On such occasions, Maurice would bundle the family into the well-aired cellar beneath the furniture showrooms with enough food to keep them going, and erect a brick wall which completely sealed them off from would-be assailants. The practice was known to several members of the congregation and arrangements made to rescue the hidden ones should

Maurice not survive the pogrom. This uncomfortable experience proved the saving of the family's lives on more than one occasion.

One Easter eve the ominous warnings came and Maurice once again walled up the family in the cellar. Unfortunately, this time the drunken mob, unable to break down the iron grille which blocked the entrance to the showrooms, decided to set fire to them – before long the place was uncontrollably ablaze. Maurice worked unceasingly to demolish the wall he had built. He released his wife and children and they escaped into the garden, where they sat watching their home and livelihood go up in smoke.

Suddenly, my grandmother gasped in panic. Where was Rachel? A moment before she had been on the grass beside them, crying for Dalia, her favourite doll, and now she was nowhere to be seen. Perhaps she'd gone back for Dalia. Maurice rushed into the building, calling her name. At the foot of the staircase which led to their flat above the showrooms, he found the bow from her hair. He raced up the blazing stairs, making for the nursery. He passed the open door of his bedroom and heard coughing. In the smoke-filled room he found a small being, crouched against a heavy chest of drawers, one of which was open. He took Rachel in his arms and returned through the flames to the garden. This feat was more perilous than it sounds, for it appears that his hair and eyebrows were singed and part of his clothing had caught fire.

The family remained in the garden the whole night, little Rachel sobbing herself to sleep because she had not saved her doll Dalia.

'To think,' Maurice said to his wife, 'only a few days ago I received two thousand roubles in notes for the sale of some furniture, and we kept the money in the house. Now it's feeding the flames. Where did you put it, Manya?'

'In the chest of drawers.'

'Which? In our bedroom?'

'Yes, Maurice.' Maurice thought back to where he had

found the child, crouched by the open drawer of the chest.
'Rachel ...' he called softly.
'Hush, Maurice. Don't wake her.'
'What is she holding so tightly in her clenched fist?'
'Probably her hankie. Don't disturb her.'

But something was troubling Maurice and he was impatient to know. He gently unclasped her fingers and there fell from her hand a small bundle of notes – the two thousand roubles her mummy had hidden in the chest of drawers in the bedroom.

Now what would have made my mother – who was then only three years old – forsake her beloved doll Dalia, for whom she had risked her life in the fire, and instead run into her parents' room, open a drawer which was normally too heavy for her to move and clutch the only liquid money the family now possessed: the two thousand roubles she did not even know existed and which later enabled her father to start up his business once again? It could be tossed off as coincidence, as luck, as 'just one of those things!' But one could also recognize something more.

CB

The Law Student

DURING THE Czar's regime in Russia, Jews had little freedom, an anxious present and a bleak future. But one possession enriched their spirit and made life bearable: their belief in God and His Law which had been handed down from generation to generation and which they felt could never be taken from them. It was the cherished hope of every father to have at least one son who would wish to study Hebrew Law and continue the tradition of his forefathers.

This study however was a dangerous occupation for it was forbidden by the Russian government and could be done only in the utmost secrecy.

A young cousin of my mother called Shalom had chosen this hazardous path, and would leave home at night to make for a house several miles away where a group of enthusiasts gathered to study under a 'Zadik' (a learned teacher). One night, Shalom embraced his wife and set out in the dark on the road he knew so well – but, after only an hour or so, he returned home. His wife questioned him anxiously and he attempted to explain.

'I reached the bridge, Leah, as usual – but, as soon as I stepped off the road, a sudden gust of wind startled me and I found myself afraid for the first time since I was a child.'

'Afraid of what?'

'That's just it … I don't know. It was uncanny. I tried to walk, but this wind was so powerful that I couldn't continue. It was as though a battering ram kept gently prodding me in the chest, to remind me of its strength if I attempted to resist it. I tried, Leah, honestly I did, but I simply couldn't get across the bridge.'

'So you came home!' mocked his wife.

'Not immediately, Leah. No, not until the voice spoke in my ear.'

'What voice?'

'I don't know. But I could swear the wind had a voice and whispered to me. It seemed to be warning me to go back. At first I told myself I was a fool to let my imagination influence me, but it was useless. I just couldn't fight it. So I gave in and returned home. Don't laugh at me.'

But his wife did laugh. She could admire a man who was prepared to risk arrest and imprisonment in order to study Hebrew Law but how could she respect one who was frightened by a strong wind which could do no more harm than blow off a man's hat or turn his cloak inside out? Each time her husband left home she had sat up in prayer, confident that he would return in the morning … and yet … unable to stifle the fear that one of these nights, his *au revoir* might prove to be an *adieu*. A chance meeting with a police officer, a tip to the authorities from a suspicious neighbour – there were many fears to occupy her mind in the waking hours – but never in her wildest dreams did she consider the possibility that he might come back without even reaching the other house, and for so paltry a reason.

Leah was concerned for what the other wives would say when they learned about it. And what of the teacher? Would he ever permit Shalom to attend class again? Would Shalom not become the object of jest, of jostling elbows and sniggering tongues? That night neither of them slept much. He, with analysing the mystery, and she, with concern for the following day.

Bad news spreads fast and in the morning Leah learned the appalling truth that, during the night, Jew-baiters had surrounded the building where the young men were studying and set fire to the house: all inside had perished. Only Shalom, her husband, remained alive.

Being an actor by profession, I may, unwittingly, have dramatized this event in the retelling of it, but the facts are true, as my mother vouched. I recall even now the sensation that came over me when I first heard the story from her: not a fear of ghosts, but a comforting realization that God proves his existence to an individual every so often – and that perhaps the voice in the wind was not after all an imagined one.

CB

The Menorah

WHEN THE century was still young and it was easier for a Jew to leave Russia than during the Communist regime, a young engaged couple in the town of Brestlitovsk decided to emigrate to America where a Jew could survive as a Jew without the constant fear of pogroms. Having saved enough money for one single fare, they decided that the lad – Ilya – would go ahead, to gather some of the legendary gold to be found on the street pavements in the New World, and, once he had sufficient, he would send for his bride.

A month later, the Jews of the town pooled their roubles and made a wedding gift to the bride of a boat ticket to join her love. She arrived in Brooklyn totally unexpected and called at the address of her fiancé – only to find that he had moved elsewhere without leaving his new address. The girl stayed in the room he had vacated while she searched for Ilya – without success. How could she trace him in a strange country, knowing not a word of English, and not a soul to turn to? Her money soon ran out, and she began to pawn her few worthwhile possessions to a Jewish pawnbroker she found nearby. Finally, she had nothing left of value other than the silver Menorah her grandmother had gifted her. With a heavy heart, she pledged that too.

Hanukah was actually upon her and, by chance, on the very eve, Ilya happened to pass by the same pawnbroker, and noticed the Menorah displayed in the window. He recognized it immediately, and could not believe his eyes. Could a duplicate possibly exist so many thousands of miles away from Russia? He entered the shop and asked about the Menorah. The pawnbroker told him that a young Russian girl had pledged it, that she was searching for her fiancé and had so far had no luck. Ilya explained that he must be that fiancé, redeemed the pledge, took her address and went straight there.

The girl was preparing the cheap candleholder she had bought for the festival, weeping at the loss of her fiancé and her beautiful silver Menorah ... when there was a knock at the door. Wiping her eyes, she opened it – and found both, plus her future, standing before her. That girl was my aunt – Manya Rosenay.

CB

I'm Your Cousin Ilya

THERE IS AN amusing story told about the Czar of Russia inspecting his troops, and stopping before a soldier every now and then to exchange a few words. 'What is your name, my good man?' he asked one.

'Abraham Cohen, Your Majesty.'

'Cohen. A Jewish name. Are you of that persuasion?'

'Yes, Your Majesty.'

'Tell me, my good man, how do you like being a soldier of your Czar?'

'Permission to speak frankly, Your Majesty?'

'Of course, why else would I ask you that?'

'Well, to tell the truth, Sire – it's diabolical. It's bad enough for an ordinary Russian – but for a Jew it's ten times worse. They mock me, steal my food, put me on the dirtiest and meanest of duties ... and honestly, Sire – it's sheer Hell!'

'My son ...' the Czar sighed, 'you have only your individual worries to concern you. Have you any idea of the troubles and worries which beset your Czar, the father of all the Russians? I share the concerns of every one of my people, from the richest to the poorest. I hardly sleep at night, worrying about how to feed and clothe my people, how to bring prosperity to my country, how to ensure that their

9

children are fed and given a chance in life. Believe me, my worries are a thousand times worse than yours.'

The soldier was moved to tears. 'I never realized that you suffered so much, Your Majesty.' He placed his hand on the Czar's shoulder, and whispered, 'I tell you what – let's you and me emigrate to America!'

Times were becoming extremely hard for my grandparents in Brestlitovsk, and Maurice Rosenay dreamt of taking the advice of that apocryphal Jewish soldier – to emigrate to America. This could not be done just out of the blue, so he chose the most intelligent of his nephews, gave him what roubles he could and the family jewels to sell and packed him off to the States to make his fortune, on the understanding that he would then send for the rest of the family.

Young Ilya arrived in New York, armed with little luggage, but with something more precious: the address of a distant relative called Mihail who had offered him a room and a job. The man was to have met him at the docks, but, as luck would have it, the ship arrived a day sooner than scheduled and he found no one to greet him in the 'golden land'.

Speaking nothing but Russian and Yiddish, he showed the address of his relative to a man who put him on a train and noted down where he should get off. Confused by the words which were in an alphabet so different from his own, he journeyed way past the station. Looking at the faces around him, he noticed one with high cheekbones and a beard, and wearing a hat. He addressed the man in Yiddish, showing him the name and address of the relative he was searching for.

The other's eyes lit up. 'But, we weren't expecting you till tomorrow! I'm your cousin Mihail!'

Ilya was industrious and within a few years, when Mihail died, he was left in charge of the business. True to his word, he sent his uncle the money for the fare to the States. It took quite a time to settle his affairs, so it was decided to emigrate in batches. My mother (who was then 12) and her aunt were sent as the forerunners. But several months had elapsed since

Ilya sent the money, and meantime the business in New York had been sold and he had moved to another district. His letter giving the new address reached Brestlitovsk after my mother had left, and, in consequence, the new arrivals were not met when the ship docked.

They stayed in a rooming house for several days while my mother's aunt tried to trace Ilya. They had been out one morning when her aunt placed her on the overhead railway, and told her to descend at the second of three bridges which was close to their apartment, and from where she knew her way home. By mistake she went beyond the stop and walked for over two hours, lost and frightened in a country where she did not understand a word. She finally sat in a doorway of a shop and cried bitterly. The owner came out to see what was wrong. To his surprise the girl spoke in Russian, his native tongue.

'What's your name, little one?' he asked.

'Rachel Rosenay,' she replied.

The shopkeeper threw open his arms. 'Let me embrace you ...' he exclaimed. 'I'm your cousin, Ilya!'

⋈

Aunt Sarah

MANY OF US, I am sure, have had a psychic experience at some time in our lives which we were unable to explain. My mother had several, and one of the most impressive concerned an incident which happened when she was ten years of age. The family had gone on holiday to the seaside and she was paddling with her young cousins when she became adventurous and wandered behind some rocks

11

and out of her depth. She struggled hard to remain above water – but it was hopeless. She was found unconscious by the water's edge. Two members of the local life-saving group gave her artificial respiration and she came to.

A few weeks later, her mother was showing her the family photo album and, among the faded sepia likenesses of grandparents she had never met and distant relatives who were but names to her, she recognized a face.

'Mamma, who's that lady?'

'That's your Aunt Sarah. Such a kind woman. She loved you dearly. She died when you were quite little, God rest her soul.'

'No, she's not dead, Mamma. That's the lady who pulled me out of the water.'

Her mother looked strangely at her and said, 'Yes, Sarah promised she'd watch after you.'

Twice since then, we nearly lost Mother. Once when my brother and I were being bathed by her, and we were all three affected by gas escaping from a faulty geyser. Mother was able to drag Ronald out of the bath, but fainted as she was trying to pull me out. Father was giving a violin lesson in the room below and, without realizing why, had a sudden urge to rush to the bathroom – in time to rescue us all. Mother was delirious that night, and the doctor said that if she came out of this delirium by the morning, she would recover. Thank Heaven she did.

'I saw Aunt Sarah last night,' she said.

On another occasion she was extremely ill, and we nearly lost her. Again, on recovering, she said, 'I saw Aunt Sarah in my sleep.'

I cannot confess to being as psychic as Mother, but I did have one encounter worth relating. I had received a sudden call to Rome to work on a film. I booked the last flight out that evening and busied myself packing my case. My brother telephoned me. 'Is it true you're flying to Rome tonight?'

'How on earth did you know, Ronald? I haven't told anyone.'

'A spiritualist friend of mine rang me to say you were off, and that I must warn you NOT to catch that plane.'

'Nonsense! I have to go tonight, and it's the last plane out. I'm to replace an actor who's fallen ill, and I have to be on the set first thing in the morning.'

His voice grew commanding as it often did when I contradicted him. 'Bob, I INSIST YOU DO AS I SAY. DON'T CATCH THAT PLANE.'

Well, I can be as obstinate as Ronald and I told him if that was all he had to say I was not interested in pursuing the conversation. I arrived in good time at London Airport, checked in my luggage, sat in the lounge, then following the other passengers to the plane. I boarded and took my seat, fastened the safety belt and accepted the boiled sweet the stewardess offered me.

The engines began to rev and the plane slowly taxied towards the runway. I could feel the tremendous power of the beautiful monster as she vibrated beneath us and I told myself that my brother's concern was undoubtedly without foundation. I glanced out of the window at the concrete, wet from the endless winter rain, and my eye caught what looked like the reflection of a face in a puddle. It was a face I did not recognize, but something within me told me, 'Aunt Sarah'.

At that moment the engines gathered speed, and the plane quivered like a race horse at the starting post. The engines cut out abruptly and there was utter silence on board. Then, the voice of the stewardess came over the speaker: 'Ladies and gentlemen, we regret that there will be an unavoidable delay in departure. Passengers are requested to leave the plane and board the coach which will convey them back to the waiting lounge.'

Later we learnt that a fault had been found in one of the engines, and we were diverted to another plane.

Jonathan

T HE INDIANS have an expression: 'The life you bear is as naught to the life you save.'

My mother has told me many anecdotes of her childhood in Russia, in Egypt and America, which have strengthened my faith in God; but none so much as the story concerning her cousin Elyahu who arrived in New York at the age of 15 with five dollars, the clothes in which he stood, a toothbrush and comb, and a burning ambition to become a doctor. He went to live with my mother's family where he shared a bed with three cousins, and increased the light bills by his studies at night.

A bright boy, he passed through school with honours and was admitted to a college of medicine. At 23, he met and married an art student. By the time he was a house physician, the young couple had one child and another on the way. To make ends meet was an ever-increasing battle, and pennies saved were as important as blood donated to a needy patient. Elyahu and Jenny made the usual economies wherever possible, including, of course, walking to and from the hospital to save bus fares.

At four o'clock one morning, he set out for home after a long stretch on duty. He normally took the shortest way but, for some unaccountable reason, this time he felt the urge to take a totally different route which meant using a road he particularly avoided – especially at night – for it was a notorious trouble spot. He was too tired to question the inner urge which brought him to this street which was narrow and flanked by ugly houses. He noticed a woman walking ahead of him step off the kerb without glancing either way. A fast-moving car coming from behind drove straight towards her without signalling or making any visible attempt to swerve. The woman was knocked down and the driver continued on his way.

A quick examination showed her to be dead. Elyahu could see too that she was pregnant. He carried her back to the hospital where he performed a Caesarian and delivered the child. Enquiries failed to establish the identity of the dead mother. In her bag was found a list of boys' and girls' names with one ringed in ink: Jonathan. And so Jonathan the baby became.

In due course the necessary formalities were completed and Elyahu and Jenny adopted the child. Jonathan eventually grew up to become an eminent eye surgeon, and among his claims to distinction is the development of a new method of maintaining the virus needed in the treatment of trachoma, which has probably saved the sight of thousands of children out in the East. They owe this debt to the 'inner voice' which forced Elyahu Rosenay to take the wrong route home at four o'clock one fateful night in New York, more than half a century ago, to bring to this world an orphaned child whose only possession was his name – Jonathan. A name which means 'gift from God'.

Cʒ

A Pound Well Spent

OF COURSE IT could be sheer luck that we find ourselves in a given place at a given time when an event occurs which changes the course of our lives. But even the least religious among us must at times wonder whether the coincidence was entirely accidental, or whether the threads of our lives don't somehow follow a pattern already designed.

My friend June Epstein exists because of a pound. Many years ago, her father – then a bachelor – was appealed to by a street beggar, and, feeling in a generous mood, he gave the man a pound. Several years later, the 1914–18 war broke out, and Epstein joined the army. He found himself in a unit which was due to be sent abroad. The sergeant of his company called him aside and told him in confidence where they were going.

'Do you want to go there?' he asked.

'Not particularly,' said Epstein.

'Well, where d'you want to go?'

'I think I'd like to go to India.'

'OK,' replied the sergeant. 'Leave that to me.'

'Why should you do this for me?' asked Epstein.

The sergeant looked oddly at him. 'You once gave a pound to a street beggar down on his luck. I was that beggar!'

In Calcutta, Epstein met a tall, smiling girl who attracted him enormously. He discovered she was the daughter of the Chief Rabbi of the city: a woman of his own faith and way of life, many hundreds of miles from his home and people. He proposed to her, and was accepted. After the war, she returned with him to London where they set up home and June was born.

That pound proved to be the best investment of Epstein's life. But was it merely the whirligig of chance? I wonder?

၈

Do You Want a Baby?

To MANY OF you, the name Gladys Aylward is not unfamiliar. She was a remarkable English woman who devoted her life to giving a home and love to hundreds of orphaned Chinese children.

One night, a boy working at Gladys's bungalow on

Formosa was returning to the orphanage when, suddenly and quite unaccountably, he felt the urge to go back. He was already a couple of miles from the bungalow, but the feeling overwhelmed him and he went back. As he unlocked the gate, his foot kicked against a bundle of rubbish wrapped in newspaper. He picked it up and made for the dustbin, when the parcel wobbled. He grasped it now with his other hand to prevent it breaking apart, and felt a face. He took the dirty parcel in to Gladys Aylward and called out, 'Ma ... do you want a baby?'

Gladys examined the bundle, and, in her own words, he was 'far from an attractive sight. He had no hair, a skin disease covered his entire body, a rupture bulged from his tummy and his asthma was so bad he was wheezing like a buzz-saw. And he was filthy!'

She was convinced he'd die in the night. But she cleaned him up with cooking oil, then rolled him in a blanket and took him to bed with her. To her amazement he survived the night, and Gladys set to work with faith and ointment and a halfpenny which she bound against the ruptured tummy.

Within two weeks the rupture had gone and the rash had improved, and for six months he made steady progress. One morning Gordon, as she called him, began suddenly to choke. He was rushed straight off to hospital and they operated. A hole was cut in his neck and he had to breathe through a tube in his throat.

Gladys slept in the hospital and nursed him herself for five months. Twice more the doctor operated but was reluctant to risk a fourth. It looked as though Gordon would live his life in a hospital bed, breathing through a tube. Gladys begged the doctor and he finally agreed to operate again on two conditions: that she assist him, and that she ask everyone she knew to pray for the boy. Gladys did this. She even sent a telegram to an old friend in England saying: 'Please pray for one baby.' (The woman was herself an invalid and she really *could* pray!)

17

The doctor operated and, after that, it was up to Gladys. She sat with Gordon, holding him upright, giving his little windpipe time to learn to work. After a few hours she felt her arms would fall off, but she wouldn't allow anyone else to hold the boy. The result? Gordon was home within a week. He is now a grown lad: a bright, laughing, intelligent boy. When he came to London, he learned to speak English in less than two months, without anybody teaching him.

Little Gordon lives only because 'something' whispered into a Chinese boy's ear and made him return two miles to pick up a dirty parcel destined, it seemed, for the dustbin. Something … or Some One?

❦

The Force of Love

THE FOLLOWING story was told me by my brother Ronald.

At a reception I attended to raise funds for a hospital in Israel, the guest of honour was a high-ranking member of the Israeli Parliament who spoke eloquently and persuasively. Many hands went to their cheque books and a generous sum was raised to buy new medical equipment, beds and an ambulance. I was very impressed with the speaker and could well understand the predictions voiced by the 'pundits' that, given a few more years of experience, the gentleman might find the path clear to the premiership.

The name of the speaker and something he said about having been a patient in that very hospital as a child stirred a distant memory, and quite suddenly I knew where I had seen him before. During my five-and-a-half years' service in the British Army in the last war and after, I had served for a short time in what was then Palestine. I had visited that hospital when it was a mere collection of huts and temporary dwellings, and in the children's ward I had noticed a boy lying asleep in a metal cot, sucking his bottle. Although he was curled up in a tight ball, as though he was attempting to relive his existence in his mother's womb, he seemed too old and too big for a baby's cot. Curious to know his malady, I glanced surreptitiously at the chart at the end of his bed – and saw only his name and the recommended treatment. It read: 'Love – every half hour'.

I asked a nurse what that meant and she explained that the boy was the sole survivor of a batch of Polish children who were found abandoned by the Nazis when their concentration camp was overrun by the British towards the end of the war. The German doctors in the camp had been conducting an inhuman experiment on the very young children: they had separated them from their mothers and kept them in confinement under the supervision of Aryan women who were forbidden ever to talk to them, to cuddle them or to show any interest whatever. This was an attempt to assess if the deprivation of love would stunt their growth and to judge how much of their normal development was due to the contact with the mother and to the love and attention given them by her.

The results were disturbing. Generally the little ones communicated with each other by animal-like noises; others never uttered a sound. Many slept too much and became lethargic, lacking all energy. Most took to cuddling themselves with their arms clasped tightly across their chests and rocked all day long either from side to side or backward and forward. Some cried or hummed throughout their waking moments, and the majority gave up the ghost and died – not through lack of food – but of the hunger for love and attention. I can think of few more inhuman experiments man could perform on a fellow-being – and a helpless, tiny, dependent human being at that.

When the British reached the concentration camp, the sole survivor of this particular batch of children was the little lad later taken to Palestine and whom I had come across in the cot in the hospital. On arrival he weighed only 11 lb, had massive pneumonia, there was a deficiency in the number of thrombocycytes and his extremities were becoming deformed. During treatment he stopped breathing, he turned blue and his heart stopped beating. He was revived by artificial respiration, at first from mouth to mouth, then with oxygen and cardiac massage. The results of lab tests showed that his body contained only 3 mg of calcium. By all the laws of nature when the serum shows under 7 mg a person usually goes into spasms and loses consciousness. It is generally accepted that one cannot live with fewer than 5 mgs of calcium. The child had survived with only 3 mgs of calcium: a rare medical phenomenon.

When I saw him, he had already recovered from most of his troubles, but was evidently attempting to catch up with what he had missed both physically and psychologically as a baby, and that was why he felt most comfortable curled up like an embryo in a cot, sucking a bottle he ought long since to have discarded.

The doctor who prescribed 'Love – every half hour' was an inspired man and the regular cuddle, coo and caress paid dividends, for that child who defeated death in the concentration camp is now one of the most eloquent ambassadors for his country, a brilliant politician and, who knows, a Prime Minister to be? Such is the force of love. Love … and something else?

☙

Little Wiranto

JEANNETTE ALWAYS had a hankering after the Orient. As a student, she travelled much and luck brought her into contact with a young Indonesian called Sueharto who possessed all that she admired most in a man. A brisk engagement blossomed into marriage, and Sueharto took Jeannette back to his own land where she learned to adapt herself to his way of life. 'Thy people shall be my people.' They both loved children and brought five sons into the world – five healthy mixtures of the Orient and Europe – with the colouring of skin and interesting features which melt the hearts of women the world over.

Political troubles are spelt with capital letters in that area of the globe, and, one early morning, police arrived at the house with orders to arrest both Sueharto and Jeannette. No mention had been made of children in their warrant, and Sueharto and Jeannette were dragged off without being given time to make any arrangements for the care of their youngsters. When the five returned later from school, it was to find wooden struts nailed across the doors and windows, and no means of entry.

Good neighbours came to their help – in no time, four of the youngsters had been taken by different families – and Sueharto's brother was on his way over to fetch Wiranto the youngest. But Wiranto was only eight and for him it was difficult to understand why his precious mummy was not at home to receive them as usual and to prepare their meal. He didn't care to be taken into another house, even though it was his uncle's; he wanted his own mummy and daddy and all the familiar things around him which spelt home. He slipped away and went in search of his parents.

At the prison, Sueharto and Jeannette were separated, and subjected to the treatment often meted out to political prisoners: no charge, no explanation, no hint of trial or reason for arrest. Just communal cells, lice-infested straw beds, the body almost starved of food and the mind left to stagnate. After two months of agonizing lack of news, a friend managed to get word through a guard that four of the five children were safe and in good hands – but that the youngest had run away. A search was being made and, if possible, they'd let her know as soon as he was found.

Imagine the torment of this young European woman: jailed for no apparent reason, left without news of her husband and worried about the children – 'Thank God four were all right' – but utter silence about her youngest who was too little to fend for himself. 'Had he been taken in by strangers? Where was he sleeping? Did he have enough to eat? Supposing he's been run over, kidnapped, fallen in the river, got totally lost … God, where was her baby, her little, cuddly, nestly, adorable little Wiranto … the most sensitive of the brood, the one who needed the most love and attention, who could not bear her to be out of her sight for long … Oh God – where is he? Please, please protect him and see that he comes to no harm.'

Three months passed, then four, then five, half a year – and still no word. Through the grapevine of the prison, Jeannette received a message of love and comfort from her husband Sueharto – he was alive and not treated too badly – but as for little Wiranto, utter silence.

Mental anguish gave way to apathy. To occupy themselves, the prisoners had formed a choir and those who could gave lessons to the others. Exercises were organized to pass the relentless days, but Jeannette sank deeper and deeper into a depressed silence which emptied her mind of hope, of prayer, or the desire for the company of others. She was slowly degenerating into a vegetable. Each day, ten of the women, accompanied by several guards, collected the garbage and were allowed beyond the prison gates to carry it to a refuse dump a mile-and-a-half away. No one was compelled to go, but all welcomed this distraction and the chance to confirm to themselves that life still existed beyond those thick walls. A roster was worked out, and each woman given a turn. But Jeannette refused to participate. She spent her days in a stupor and her nights in the heavy sleep of those whose minds are numbed.

One particular morning, she broke her silence and for no apparent reason announced that she wanted to join her companions on the garbage trek that day. One woman grudgingly gave up her turn, and Jeannette breathed the outside air for the first time in nine months. On their way back from the refuse dump, she noticed a child about a hundred yards ahead bending to pick up something from the street which he conveyed to his mouth. She needed no prompting to recognize the familiar shape.

She screamed and broke away from the group. The guards shouted and gave chase; the frightened child took to his heels. By now all the women followed, yelling his name. They caught up with the boy, and Jeannette fell to her knees, her little bundle of love and flesh clasped tight in her arms. When they had both given vent to enough tears and pent up emotions Jeannette was able to examine her son. He was painfully thin and very, very dirty. Since the day he had gone in search of his mother, the child had existed on scraps of food found in dustbins, scrounged from strangers, or simply stolen. He had not washed, changed his clothes or slept in a bed. Recently he had teamed up with a gang of child thieves who had taught him how to pick pockets and beg professionally, and as a result he had had a little more to eat. The guards winked and Jeannette was able to take Wiranto back to prison and secrete him in the women's cell. Mother and son began to climb the path to normality again.

Meanwhile, Jeannette's brother-in-law had been in contact with the British Embassy: the right strings were jerked and Jeannette was released as suddenly as she'd been arrested. Eventually she managed to return to England with the children – but in the many years since then she had received only occasional word from her husband who still languished in prison without charge or trial.

There are perhaps hundreds of similar tales to tell of that strife-torn country. But, sometimes, in the ugliness, the cruelty and the apparent inhumanity, a finger points in a certain direction and those who follow it recognize Whose hand guides that finger. One such woman was Jeannette who awoke from her torpor after nine months of slow dying, and followed that finger which led her to her lost child. That same hand closed its protective palm around them and conveyed them to the safety of our shores. Let us hope the finger will not forget her husband Sueharto and the scores of other unfortunate beings who are suffering through man's inhumanity to man.

ଔ   ଔ   ଔ

This true story was told me by Miriam Brickman – a well-known film casting-director – and the sister of Jeannette.

ଔ

Together

MY MOTHER Rachel, may she rest in peace, used to suffer badly from arthritis, and, early in the last world war she was sent to Buxton for spa treatment. In the hospital was a Polish immigrant who spoke no English and seemed extraordinarily lonely. Roman had escaped from Poland and made his way across Europe and the Channel to join the scores of refugees who sought succour and a new life on our hospitable shores. During his escape he had lost his wife whom he had not seen now for three years, but an inner voice and faith told him she was alive and would one day arrive in England to join him.

My mother busied herself trying to lighten his worries, and pointed out that the cook happened to be Polish and could converse with Roman and interpret his requests to the nurses. Roman accompanied her to the kitchen, and gave a scream which penetrated the very marrow of mother's bones – the Polish cook was none other than his lost wife, Stefania!

There is an old Jewish saying: 'God creates them – and brings them together.' He certainly did on that day in Buxton, for Roman and Stefania.

08

Return to the Fold

MY FRIEND Ephraim Kestenbaum often journeys to the United States on business and, whenever possible, he makes a point of contacting the local Jewish community. On one such trip he was in a small town which seemed devoid of Jews. In the telephone directory he found two listings who might have been 'sons of Abraham'. He took a chance and called at the home of the first family. He was well received and treated with the customary American hospitality by Mr Silverstone. At an opportune moment, Ephraim pointed out that a Jewish school existed in the neighbouring township and perhaps the man would consider sending his children there. His host abruptly changed attitude. 'I am not a "Yid",' he said, 'and even if there had ever been Jewish forebears in the family, I would not want my daughter to know of it.' He drew Ephraim to the window and pointed to a child playing with her school chums nearby. 'That's my little girl. She's a full-blooded American. And that's what I want her to be.'

Later, Ephraim called on the second family who immediately acknowledged their religion and lamented the fact that they knew of no other Jews in the neighbourhood. Ephraim gave them the same information he had imparted to the others, and the news was treated with relish and the promise that their children would be enrolled in the Jewish school.

On his way to the station, Ephraim happened to meet the little daughter of Mr Silverstone and she greeted him in a disarmingly friendly manner. 'What's your name?' she asked.

'Mine is Ephraim. What's yours?'

'I'm Abigail.'

'That's a lovely name, Abigail.'

'Well, I've a lovely mummy and daddy. Will you come home to tea and meet them?'

'I'm so sorry … I'm on my way to the station.'

'Oh please, do come home with me … just for a little while. I'm sure my mummy and daddy would like to know you. You're such a nice man.'

'I'll tell you what … when I come back, a little later today, about 5.30, I'll call at your house … but promise me you'll ask them first. Tell them my name and how we met, and ask if it's all right for me to call. Promise?'

'I promise. But make sure you come before I go to bed. I ll be watching television in the room above the front door, so call out my name and I'll come to the window. If I put up my thumb it means it's OK. OK?'

'OK,' said Ephraim, and he kept his word. At half past five, he stood outside Abigail's home and called out her name. The little girl leaned out of the window.

'I told Mummy and Daddy how we met and they are happy for you to come to tea. They're expecting you now. Just ring the door bell.'

Ephraim was nervous of paying a second visit so soon after

his not too pleasant encounter with Abigail's father earlier in the day, but he need not have worried. He was given a warm welcome, and when he next visited the neighbouring town, some four months later, to his delight he found that not only was Abigail enrolled in the Jewish school, but her parents were now members of the congregation and attended the synagogue.

It could have been mere coincidence that Ephraim happened to be in the same street as Abigail when she caught his eye and invited him home. Of course it could. But it could also have been something else …

Part II
The Small Miracles

'In Israel – miracles are an everyday occurrence.
It is the day-to-day events which are difficult.'

Moshe Dayan

Small Miracles

WE ARE ASTONISHED by the great miracles of which we read in the Bible; but when we pause to consider the little manifestations which occur all the time around us, do they really appear any less miraculous?

Who as a child has not been terrified by a storm, by a fierce dog, by the intensity of the dark, by a situation beyond our control? And who has not been comforted as a result of those three words, thrust, perhaps unconsciously, from the depths of our being out into the vast spaces between us and the beyond: those simple monosyllables, 'God help me'? When those words appear to have been heard and answered, the comforted person is often aware that he alone could not have brought about the thing he prayed for. But what of those who later hear of these 'trivialities'? Must they consider only spectacular results as emanating from Him, and the little adjustments of our problems as mere coincidence?

I remember as a boy returning from school one afternoon being caught in a sudden deluge which penetrated through to my skin and scared me beyond belief. Nothing frightened me more than thunder and lightning and on all previous occasions there was always my mother close by to run to and nestle against – an unceasing source of love to dispel my concern. This time I was alone in the street. No mother and no help. My tears joined the rain on my face as I cried, 'Please help me!' Within seconds the downpour had ceased as abruptly as it had started. I was able to reach home before the clouds opened up again in their liquid anger. How trite to attribute that to God. And yet?

In 1942, while the war was on, Ria Mendel who now lives not far from my home, had returned to her London flat to change into her best clothes in order to keep perhaps the most important date of her young life: her soldier boyfriend was being drafted abroad and had something important he wanted to say to her. Bells of delight and anticipation rang in her ears as she opened her handbag and fumbled for the keys. There were two locks on the front door and to her dismay she realized she had only one of the keys with her. The second languished on a ring she had left in her other handbag in the country house where her family had taken refuge from the bombing.

What to do? She dared not go to meet Pat dressed in her travelling clothes, feeling hot and sticky and without washing her hair. 'Why not?' I personally would ask. But then I'm a mere man. Such things which are of indifference to the male are desperately important to a girl who is about to become engaged.

Sobbing with anger and frustration Ria tried the various odd keys she had with her, knowing already that only the key specially cut for the security lock could possibly open that door. 'Oh God … Oh God,' she muttered to herself. One of the keys entered the keyhole and, with a familiar click, opened the door.

Ria kept her appointment, looking her best, and her boyfriend became her fiancé and later her husband. Yet, that same key which 'opened sesame' to her prayer and her predicament never again manoeuvred the lock. It would not even enter the keyhole.

Nikolaus Hatzitetrou lives just outside Athens. He earns his living by buying fruit and vegetables direct from the farmers and transporting his load by mule cart to town before the sun has ascended high into the sky. He tries to avoid halting the mule, for the animal is as unpredictable as he is obstinate and there is no knowing if he will accept the command to start up again with his heavy load once has has tasted the sweet, cool water of the stream or known the luxury of a brief rest in the shade.

However, one morning, the heat was so intense and Nikolaus's thirst so pressing that he was forced to pause a few moments to quench it. He sat on the protruding root of a tree beneath the shelter of its branches and bit deep into a juicy watermelon, when he heard a cry which seemed to come from under his feet. Nikolaus looked around. There was no one in sight. He shrugged his shoulders and was about to take a second bite when he heard that cry again. A thin, faint wail. Again, it seemed to come from under the ground. Nikolaus dropped his watermelon and in terror ran along the road until he reached a telephone booth.

The policeman who answered the phone was sceptical as Nikolaus – hot, out of breath and still terrified – told his story. But a routine investigation was ordered. Nikolaus took the police back to the spot where he had dropped the watermelon and the police began to dig. Three feet down they found a newly-born girl, wrapped in a newspaper, her hands and feet tied with string. She was still alive. The baby was rushed to hospital. Soon she was crying lustily, none the worse for her brush with death.

Doctors said she was about 24 hours old and had probably spent 12 hours underground. Three things, they said, had helped to keep her alive: the newspaper which had protected her face, the warm temperature of the sun-baked earth and the lumpy soil which let sufficient air through for her to breathe. But was there not also a fourth?

CȜ

That's All I Asked For

TWO OF MY best friends in Italy were Gualtiero and Beryl Tumiati. In his time, Gualtiero had been a lawyer, an actor-manager, the first Italian to translate the less familiar plays of Shakespeare and, for a score or more years, was considered Italy's greatest classic actor. He married an English painter, Beryl Hight, who designed his sets and costumes and they toured Italy with their own company. Beryl had only one lung, and in her middle years she developed asthma. In the intense Roman heat her breathing became laboured and painful. She lost weight as a trapped lizard sheds its tail. If she could not see death beside her, she could certainly smell his presence.

When he was 78, Gualtiero entered an eye hospital. His sight was failing. A young specialist was anxious to try a new treatment which did not succeed, and Gualtiero returned home – totally blind. During his absence, Beryl had not once visited him. Excusing her inability on account of a necessary few weeks in the mountain air, the family doctor had withheld from Gualtiero the truth about his wife's state of health. She was dying. On his return, Gualtiero found Beryl confined to her bed, propped up with pillows. The life that remained in her did so solely to enable her to bid farewell to her husband. The doctor faced Gualtiero with the facts. He must be prepared for the worst.

Ever a practical man, Gualtiero sat at Beryl's side and took her hand in his. 'Beryl,' he told her, 'you have been a good wife to me, and in all these years you have never once failed me. My affliction is a curse from which I can't escape. You are a religious woman: speak with your God. I need you now more than He does. Since when did He need more dead? Explain to Him. Perhaps He'll listen.'

These words which, according to Beryl, were spoken

without sentimentality and without emotion, touched her more than she could say. She wept till the lack of breath almost choked her. Then, in silence, she prayed. Gualtiero continued to hold her hand, and she swore she felt the power of her tall, forceful, blind partner entering her. Her body seemed to gain new strength as though he – and Another – were willing her to live.

Sixteen years later, I visited them in their top-floor flat in Rome. Now almost 82, Beryl was desperately frail, her breathing was painful and she had not left the flat for four years. She continued to paint and had exhibited and won prizes in many contests. With humour she claimed she asked God for a new lease of life, and He simply gave it to her.

'It was a miracle,' I said to her.

She smiled. 'Well, only a small one. But then that's all I asked for.'

೫

The Column of Fire

DURING THE desert fighting in the last Israeli–Arab conflict, the American reporter W. Stevenson unearthed an extraordinary incident.

A corporal with no special awareness of religion said he was riding in a half-track with the regimental commander of an armour unit when he saw a tremendous fire leap up, directly in their path. The corporal called out to the commander, but he could see nothing. Thinking the officer's sand goggles were covered in dust (which was hardly surprising, as it was the commander's practice to ride with his head exposed above the turret of the tank in order to view the situation better and thereby make crack decisions and alterations to plans), the corporal called out to him to swerve aside.

Although the officer could see nothing unusual ahead, he knew his corporal well enough to trust his judgment if he were convinced of danger, so he ordered the driver to swing right into another opening which appeared between the sand-dunes. The rest of the unit followed. Only a jeep, driving at great speed almost parallel with the leading half-track and blinded by the whirling sand, motored on.

Moments after the column had changed direction, the corporal turned to where he had seen the column of flames, and, to his amazement, he could see nothing. At that very moment an explosion shook the entire area – and the straying jeep rose into the air in a hundred pieces. It had driven straight into an enemy minefield.

ɔȝ

Charlie

SINCE TIME immemorial, men have had visions which have confirmed their hopes or ambitions or spurred them on to greater efforts – or even changed their very nature and character. Today, science tends to look most sceptically on anybody's claim to have seen or been in contact with the Almighty or His emissaries in the unknown beyond which surrounds or awaits us. Various tangible terms are now used to describe the phenomenon: hysteria, neurosis, simple imagination or daydreams. The fact remains that lives have been saved, predictions made which have come to pass, 'evil' turned into 'good' by visions – be they imaginary or genuine – and it is less important to probe into their authenticity than to appreciate their effects.

A man I know had spent a few months in jail where one of the inmates (we'll call him Charlie) was an inveterate thief. His habits were horrifying and his language managed to disgust even his hardened companions. Charlie had been jailed for his part in a robbery in which his cut was £4,000. The money had never been traced, but Charlie was now paying for his sin with a stiff prison sentence. His wife and children were left penniless and relied on public assistance. Out of a pittance his wife managed to save just enough money for the fares to visit Charlie once every two months. Her tears and supplication proved of little avail. Charlie was as keen as ever to 'get even' with the hateful justice which had deprived him of his liberty and which he considered had no reason to punish him for having stolen from the rich. This was after all, his due and he would continue to take every similar opportunity in the future. One thing only he promised his wife: he alone knew the whereabouts of the £4,000 and when the time came for his release, he would make a rich woman of her. She'd have furs and crocodile handbags, the children would have decent shoes and clothes and they'd have that holiday in the sun he'd been promising them for the last ten years.

But things don't always work out as planned – even for Charlie. The Chaplain of the prison had made various attempts to reform him, but it was useless. As he gazed from the pulpit on Sunday at his all-male congregation and noticed Charlie seated among them, he must have thought to himself, 'What a victory it would be if that warped mind could only look into his own soul and allow itself to be affected by the purity which God plants in the very core of each one of us and which Charlie had surrounded with impenetrable blindness.' But what was the use even of hoping? Miracles are events one reads about. Who actually experiences them? Who?

The man who told me this story was sitting next to Charlie in the chapel and quite suddenly he saw Charlie

37

shield his eyes with his arms and stagger out of the chapel like a drunkard. After the sermon he found Charlie seated by the wall, his face pale, his mind deep in thought.

'What happened, Charlie? Did an angel strike you blind?' he asked jestingly.

Charlie glanced at him, his eyes misty with puzzlement. 'Maybe, Fred. Maybe. While the Chaplain was talking I suddenly felt my eyes dragged over to look at the painting on the side wall – and I swear that a figure like the Almighty suddenly appeared on it … all vivid green. It was so bright I couldn't look at it anymore, and I got out of the chapel, quick. Funny! Very funny!'

The story spread rapidly and Charlie became the laughing stock of the prison. But his mates could not help noticing that Charlie's language had ceased to be vile, that since that famous Sunday he had not instigated a single brawl and had even gone out of his way to help a fellow prisoner who had hurt himself at work. 'Charlie's changed!' ran the catch-phrase. And indeed, he had.

He asked the Chaplain to arrange for him to receive confirmation, but before this event, he requested an interview with the Governor in the presence of the Chaplain and insisted on seeing the police as he had something heavy on his conscience. His request was granted and Charlie confessed to where he had hidden the £4,000 he had stolen: inside an old upright piano in a public house in the north of London.

The money was retrieved and Charlie eventually left prison, a reformed character. He moved to a council flat in another district, took a steady job and commenced an entirely new life: clean, decent, a good husband and a good father. Imagine what he could have done with the £4,000 had he kept it. But imagine too how much more he is worth to his family, to society and above all to himself, without the money which was never his, but with a clear conscience.

The Tree

'PLEASE GOD, next year in Jerusalem.' That prayer has been uttered by most practising Jews for over two thousand years. To some it is merely lip-service, but, to those Russian Jews who sent their sons to Palestine to build farms and reclaim the land which had been ravaged and then neglected for hundreds of years, these words were full of meaning.

One such dreamer was my maternal grandfather, Moshe Rosenay. But he did more than send his sons. At the age of 45 he sold his flourishing furniture store in Brestlitovsk and emigrated with his wife and five children to the Holy Land. He bought a small plot of land and turned his dream into reality.

However, after only a few months, the 1914–18 war broke out and the position of the Jews in Palestine became difficult under the dominion of the Turks. America brought strong pressure to bear on the Turkish government and sent battleships into the harbour at Haifa to relieve the country of its unwanted Jews. Moshe packed his belongings yet again and took his family on board. The Bible commands the Jew to plant trees when he comes into a new land, especially His land, and it was Moshe's deepest regret that he had been too ill on arrival in Palestine to plant even a single sapling.

The family disembarked at Alexandria in Egypt where a welfare organization housed them in two rooms and discussed what was to be done next. In his generosity, the American President offered refuge to a certain number of these wanderers and Moshe insisted that his sons accept. 'My children,' he told them, 'our life savings have gone with the land we bought and lost in Palestine. I have nothing left to offer you. May America now be YOUR promised land. When you have prospered, send for your mother and your sister and for me. Now go – with my blessing.' What Moshe did not tell them was that his lungs were dying and he knew that he would never leave Egypt. Soon information came that his daughter Rachel (later, my mother) had been allocated a berth on another ship bound for the United States. He accepted on her behalf.

The night before leaving, Rachel lay awake in her bed next to the open door of her parents' room and heard her father whispering: 'I shall miss my Rachel terribly. I haven't long to go, Miriam, and there won't be one child left to see me to my rest.'

In the morning my mother became stubborn and resolute. She refused to leave. Moshe grew weaker and was rushed off to hospital. Mother was only 15 and was forbidden to go near him, but she insisted on staying close to his bed to attend to his needs, thereby risking her own life. Two weeks later he died.

Now comes the strange part of my story. You may have read the announcement in the press that a forest was to be planted in Israel in commemoration of the young men who died in the war. It was to be called 'The Forest of Peace'. People were invited to subscribe towards trees in their own name or individuals of their choosing.

Through the years I have had frequent contact with the Italian side of my family, but seldom given a thought to the Russian half. Out of the blue, one night I found myself thinking of my maternal grandfather. In the morning I wrote to the organizers and requested that a dozen trees be planted in his name in the Forest of Peace. When I called on my mother later that day, she told me she had dreamed of her father during the night and he had said to her: 'I am lonely. You have not been to visit me for so long. Please bury me in Israel, Rachel.' The dream had been so vivid that Mother was deeply disturbed. Curious at this strange coincidence, I enquired the whereabouts of the Forest of Peace and – it is almost impossible to believe – the plot my grandfather had originally bought and lived in for so short a time, proved to be part of the very forest now being planted.

Sheer coincidence? Or could it be that the Great Planter Himself had had a hand in the rooting of those saplings? Who knows? There is an old Jewish saying: 'At the birth of a child and the death of a man … a tree shall grow.' Your tree has been planted, Moshe Rosenay, and in spirit you have returned to Jerusalem. May you rest in peace, my grandfather.

℃ℨ

A Billion to One

IF I HAD NOT met him myself I might never have believed his story. It began in Warsaw in 1939 when the city was overrun by the Nazis. Moshe Czernaski was a young bank clerk. He was happily married to an attractive girl of his own age, Rebecca, and they had a fair-haired daughter called Katya. Warsaw suffered greatly at the hands of its conquerors, and perhaps the hardest hit were the Jews. Moshe and his family were herded with the others into the Ghetto, to be starved out of existence.

One day, coming back to their single room, Moshe found it deserted. In their periodic 'round-up' the Germans had cordoned off the block, ordered everyone on to the street and marched them off to the sealed cattle trucks which took them to the concentration camp. Moshe did not hear again of his wife and child. He joined the underground force and fought in the last stand of the Ghetto. He survived the massacre, the enslavement, the extermination, and finally regained his freedom with the liberation of Poland.

For months he searched for his family, for months he made every possible enquiry through the Red Cross and the records of the Polish and German camps. Nothing. Then he met a man who claimed to have seen his wife and child in Auschwitz. The man said they had met their deaths in the gas chamber.

Moshe closed that chapter of his life. He couldn't bear the city which held so many memories, so he journeyed to America. He changed his name to Maurice Korwin, rebuilt his life and prospered. When he was 50 he was enviably successful and respected by the staff of the business he had created in Boston. Moshe had no photograph of his lost ones, but locked in his soul was the recollection of a girl of 22 whose smile was like the sunlight and a fair-haired child whose laughter still echoed in his mind.

One day, acting on impulse, he packed a bag and flew to Israel. He joined the sightseers at the tomb of David; he paid homage to the holy places; he saw men reclaiming the barren desert and making it a fertile land. But every fair face and every eager laugh tore at a deep wound within him, till he could no longer recall the features of his loved ones, and every new face was their face and every new voice was their voice.

In Jerusalem, he met a new immigrant who spoke only Polish. They liked each other and spent many happy hours together. She wouldn't talk about her past life: she lived only for tomorrow. Like most new arrivals, she had adopted a Hebrew name: Naomi. The fact that Maurice was more than twice her age did not seem to matter. Soon he realized that if he returned to Boston, neither his prosperous business nor his comfortable way of life could make up for his newly awakened feelings for Naomi – and so Maurice posed the question. Naomi was touched. This older man who treated her with such tenderness and respect seemed to offer her the strength and purpose she needed. She too felt drawn to him, and she accepted his proposal on one condition: that her mother should join them first.

Now this was no easy task for Naomi herself had left

Poland through underground channels. But wheels were set in motion and eventually her mother managed to leave the country. Maurice went with Naomi to meet her at Haifa. On the quayside he shared her excitement when she saw her mother. As the two fell into each other's arms, his pleasure in their reunion was not without its tinge of envy.

At last Naomi freed herself from her mother and introduced Maurice. The older woman studied him closely, and then she turned pale. She said in Polish: 'Moshe ... it's you!'

'Rebecca ... Rebecca!' Slowly his arms outstretched – and man and wife held each other for the first time in 26 years.

A billion to one chance! Chance? I wonder!

&

A Lady of Faith

RABBI SMITH OF Chicago told me a remarkable story. About two months before the State of Israel was declared, he travelled there by boat on which he met a sprightly woman of 90-odd whom he saved from an accident as she nearly fell down a stairway on board ship. They exchanged the usual pleasantries which occur between travellers.

'Where are you from?'

'Chicago.'

'I, too. Are you travelling alone?'

'Yes.'

'Where to?'

'To Eretz Israel. Where else?'

'But where in Palestine?'

'I don't know. To Eretz Israel.'

'You have to know to which town you're going, otherwise the British authorities might not even let you off the boat.'

'I don't know. Just to Eretz Israel.'

'Have you any relatives there?'

'I've got a nephew.'

'Where does he live?'

'Eretz Israel.'

'But where in Eretz Israel?'

'I told you – in Eretz Israel. I don't know exactly where.'

'What's his name?'

'Chaim Szokoll.'

'Does he know you're coming?'

'No. He has never seen me before.'

Rabbi Smith looked at the old lady in wonder. 'But how will you find him?'

'I have faith in God.'

'But, Madam … the British are very tough on immigrants. If you are not expected and there's no one to meet you they might send you to a camp in Cyprus.'

'Listen, young man. I am 91 years of age – and the good Lord has never failed me yet. He'll look after me.'

In the presence of such simple, honest faith, one ceases to argue. Rabbi Smith held his peace.

Members of the Irgun had just blown up a ship which was due to be sent to Cyprus with hundreds of refugees destined to be interned and the British army was on the alert. When the ship carrying Rabbi Smith reached harbour, soldiers came on board with fixed bayonets, and everyone was ordered to have their papers ready and to alight one at a time as their name was called out. Almost like running the gauntlet, each passenger had to pass between two rows of soldiers followed by one whose bayonet was held at the ready.

Came Rabbi Smith's turn. He was not permitted to wait and accompany Mrs Szokoll, so he took leave of her, feeling greatly concerned for the old lady. Half way down the gangway, he turned to speak to her, but was immediately

prodded by the bayonet. 'Oh no, you don't – move forward!'
said the soldier.

As his feet touched soil, a young man approached him.
'Rabbi Smith? I heard your name called out. I'm a newspaper
reporter and my boss sent me to interview you.'

'Not here, young man – with a bayonet at my back. Give
me your phone number. I'll ring you when I get to my hotel
and arrange an appointment.'

'OK. I'll write it down for you.'

Rabbi Smith glanced at the piece of paper the other man
handed him and read the name Szokoll.

'Is your first name Chaim, by any chance?'

'Yes. How did you know?'

'Do you have an aunt living in Chicago?'

The other knit his brows in concentration. 'I think so, but
she must be very ancient. Who knows if she's even alive
now?'

'She's very much alive – she'll be following me down this
gangway any minute now. Just you wait.'

At that moment, over the tannoy came the announcement
of the next passenger's name, and, aided by a helpful Tommy,
Mrs Shoshana Szokoll, aged 91, stepped off the boat – into
the waiting arms of her astonished nephew Chaim Szokoll.
The Lady of Faith looked in the direction of Rabbi Smith and
smiled as she called out: 'I told you He wouldn't fail me!'

 G3

Mutti

'MOSHE, I KNOW we can't really afford it, but I feel we
must do something for those orphans they've saved
from the Nazis. Don't be angry … I know we've hardly
enough for ourselves, and it's not fair to expect you to work

yourself to the bone to feed yet another mouth ... but I always remember what my mother used to say "each child brings his own mazzel – his own luck"!'

That was Raquel speaking to her husband in Jerusalem, and far from being angry or reproaching her, Moshe said: 'Very well, Raquel – let's go to the orphanage and choose a daughter.'

'No, Moshe. You know me: I'd break down and cry and want to adopt them all ... and that would be disaster. You go alone.'

Moshe laughed. 'All right, Raquel. For my pocket's sake I'll go on my own, but you realize we'll have to tighten our belts a notch or two.'

Raquel was not put out. 'Hashem will provide.'

Both of them had bitter memories of the Jew-baiting in Hitler's early days back home in Germany and had so often reproached themselves for not doing more to persuade Raquel's parents and sister to leave Germany with them when they crossed the border on that bitter December night. But her father, always the optimist, had believed that the German people would not suffer Hitler for long, and besides, he couldn't bear to leave his furniture business which he had built up from a market barrow to the most important store in town. Now, mother, father, sister, her sister's husband and children ... all were ashes scattered in the pits of the gas chambers.

'If only I could have had children of my own,' Raquel sighed, 'but it was not to be. Some of us must be barren to counterbalance the population explosion.'

Moshe caught the bus to the building where the orphan children were housed temporarily, while Raquel busied herself preparing the corner of the living room which she screened off into a mini-bedroom for the little girl Moshe would bring home to lighten their lives. Raquel scrubbed the floors, hung the new curtains, bought flowers and splashed her housekeeping money on a beautiful roast chicken while her heart beat fast and her fingertips tingled like an actress's before a first night. Several hours later, Moshe returned. With him were not just one but two children.

'Moshe ... what have you done, for Heaven's sake? We can barely afford one ... what made you bring two?' Raquel demanded.

'Raquel, don't be cross. I couldn't help it. When I saw the girl, I somehow felt she was absolutely right for us; but the snag was that she had a brother, and I just couldn't bring myself to part them. If you'd seen how they held on to each other, you'd have done the same. I just had to take them both.'

'But Moshe ... how will we be able to feed them?'

Moshe smiled. 'Didn't your mother always say "each child brings his own luck"?'

Raquel was truly worried. She embraced the children, gave them each a plate of hot soup, then sat them on a sofa and, having no toys or children's games, gave them the family photo album to thumb through while she took Moshe into the bedroom to face him with realities.

'Moshe, it's just not possible. They're lovely children, but on your salary it's out of the question. To begin with, we've no room in the flat for two more and who can afford a bigger place? How are we to feed and clothe them both? You must have been mad even to think of it. You'll just have to take them back to the orphanage and find us ...' Raquel broke off her sentence as from the other room came a frightening scream.

They both dashed into the room – to find the little girl pointing to a photograph in the family album and crying uncontrollably, 'Mutti ... Mutti ...'. The photo was of Raquel's sister who had perished in Auschwitz.

Somehow – on that day of joy in the outskirts of the old city of Jerusalem – a city which had known death and resurrection so many times since David chose it for his capital centuries ago – Moshe Greenberg had faced a sea of worried orphans and had selected the very children of his wife's sister. It was as though the Hand of God had pointed the finger … and smiled.

൦ଃ

In Haifa Bay

'PLEASE SIR, may I have the day off to go to Haifa?'
'Why?'
'Because I have to meet the boat coming in.'
'Whatever for?'
'I'm not sure, but something inside me tells me I must.'
Joseph Millienu had escaped from Rumania at a time when it was dangerous to be a Jew, and had worked in the orange groves in Israel while piecing together the threads of his broken life. But his happiness in reaching the Promised Land would never be complete until his wife Iliena managed to join him. When they were escaping, she had fallen off the lorry in which they hid, and he had been unable to prevent her discovery and arrest as the lorry crashed through the barrier and crossed the border under gunfire. That was five years ago, and he had not heard a word from or about Iliena in all that time. He did not know of her broken leg, of her hospitalization, of the five years prison sentence. He knew only that, on this day, an inner compulsion made it necessary for him to go to Haifa to meet the boat.

As it came into the bay, the deck was overflowing with its human cargo of refugees heaped together like bandages on lint. The people alighted and were met by officials who guided them from trestle-table to trestle-table, documented them, numbered them and placed them in trucks which took them to the tents and improvised accommodation in the transit camps. One thousand per day were arriving from the Arab lands alone, plus those from Eastern Europe. All had to be housed, fed, cared for by a new government in a new yet ancient land, *their* land: poverty-stricken, short of every necessity of life, yet happy with the pangs of rebirth of the Jewish nation.

Iliena knelt and kissed the earth, as did many of the others around her: but she obstinately refused to join the queues at the trestle-tables to give her details and be sent on to the overnight camp. 'Meine Mann ... Meine Mann ist hier ...' was all she would say.

The more the officials cajoled, pressed and begged, the stronger became her resistance. She looked around the waiting relatives and curiosity-laden people who jammed the quayside, but to no avail.

Meantime, Joseph had arrived late at the dock and missed the alighting passengers. He pushed his way through the throng – staring, searching, scrutinizing.

Suddenly a cry rose above the din and the tears of embracing relatives: 'Iliena ...!'

'Joseph ... Meine Mann!'

That particular day in Israel, fate had grasped Joseph's hand and drawn him to the harbour, while stretching out its other hand to carry across hostile lands, onto an unseaworthy boat crammed to overcapacity, a woman old before her time, scarred with beatings, skinny with the starvation rations meted out in prison. But this was a woman with determination and certainty in her heart, and fate had thrust them together to complete the broken jigsaw of their lives. On that day, in Haifa Bay, there was performed yet another unexplained miracle as love re-flowered on the soil of Eretz Israel.

 С8

Back to Your Barrack Room

ALMOST EVERY other man you meet in Israel has an interesting tale to tell: a tale of survival. Menachem had been in a Polish concentration camp under the Nazis and had made a pledge that, should he see the end of the dark tunnel, he would study to become a Rabbi and devote his life to teaching the young the meaning of faith, for faith alone had prevented others saying Kaddish for him.

He had witnessed so many of his companions being singled out for the one-way ticket to the gas chambers, and each time he wondered why he had been spared. Far from elation, it gave him a feeling of guilt. The day finally came when he heard his name on the roll-call and he knew that death had to be faced with dignity. He prepared himself calmly, but could not account for the strangest feeling in his veins that, for him, this day would not end in ashes.

Outside the door to the 'final solution' he stood naked among the other men. His neighbour, Michael, spoke bitterly, blaming Hashem for not showing His hand and permitting the endless slaughter of His 'chosen people'.

'How can you be so calm, Menachem? Why don't you scream or curse, damn you?' he asked.

'That would be offering up nails for my coffin, Michael. I have faith and even as I walk through the door, I shall not lose hope.'

Michael laughed bitterly. 'There you go again with your religious humbug! I tell you, God doesn't care any longer _. and you'll soon be proving that for yourself!'

Menachem stared back at the other. 'Are you so sure, Michael?' At that moment, a German sergeant arrived with fresh orders and called out the names of three men who were told to return to barracks. One of them was Menachem.

Michael perished that day, but Menachem never discovered why he and two others were plucked back for survival. But then he doesn't question the actions of the Almighty. He merely recognizes His Hand in that moment of mercy. Every time he loses patience or faces an unfair situation, he casts his mind back to the reading of the three names and to that instant when the Divine Fishing Rod caught him on Its hook and cast him back on dry land.

☙

The Survivor

I MET HIM IN Israel: a sturdy sun-tanned senior citizen of a kibbutz where he had devoted his ingenuity to discovering how to grow plants and vegetables in the air without the need of soil, using a chemical spray and water. His arm bore the number affixed to his flesh by the Nazis in Germany. I took out my notebook and pencil and asked him if he'd be willing to tell me of his sufferings there.

He stared at me and said firmly: 'No, I will not tell you of suffering, but of death. Death and resurrection. When the Germans realized they were losing the war, rather than release us from the concentration camp, we were taken on a forced march hundreds of miles into the interior. Many of us died on the march, but still they made the rest trudge on. I was young then, and considered a strong worker, so the commandant was keen to keep me alive. But he was a sadist and took delight in singling me out for punishment on any pretext he could think of.

'Once I dared to beg him to stop beating an old man who had stumbled and could not rise. ·

'"I have not filled my quota of whip lashes today," he

laughed, "so you may take your choice, Jew. Either I give it to him, or YOU can feel the sting. Which is it to be?" He knew what my answer would be ... and he struck me across the face and chest in vicious delight.

'Day after day, when he wanted to punish an individual, he'd order me to step up and take the beating in the other's stead. In the end I could take it no longer. I begged him to shoot me there and then and put an end to it.

"You're not worth wasting a good bullet, Jew. Lie down on the road in front of that tank coming down the road and end your life yourself!"

'There was, in fact, a column of tanks coming in our direction. I limped to the centre of the road and lay down directly in the path of the leading tank. I said, "Shema Yisrael " and closed my eyes, praying for the end to be quick. I finished the Shema and I could hear the tanks passing, but I dared not open my eyes. I carried on saying any prayer I could remember. Somehow I didn't dare stop. Finally, when I looked up, I realized that they had all passed. What must have happened was the first tank commander - seeing my body on the road - had swung his tank in a curve to avoid me, and all the others must have followed his lead.

'When I realized that Hashem had inspired the commander to a merciful deed I was determined to repay His goodness by deserving the life He gifted me. I had been closer to death with each tank, and survived. It was like lying in the path of eternity, and being resurrected! From that day, nothing the commandant did could break my spirit, and he eventually tired of bothering.

'I survived the war, was rescued by the Americans ... and here I am to prove it. Now write your story and leave me in peace. I have work to do. Shalom, young man.'

ॐ

Love Thine Enemy

I T S A BEAUTIFUL sentiment, but is it really possible to love thine enemy in this day and age? To Signora Heinke Piattelli it is. This is the story of a remarkable woman and the events which led to her forgiving perhaps the greatest crime of all: murder.

The man whose path crossed hers so fatefully was born in Belgium in 1934. Raphael Blitz was only six years old when the Nazi armies invaded the country. His father was arrested and taken to a labour camp from which he never returned. In order to save her boy's life, Raphael's mother had him baptized and cared for in a convent. They had been very attached and little Raphael missed his mother desperately. She was sent for and handed back the child. Without her he was wasting away. There followed months of hiding, of moving from district to district, of anxious nights in damp cellars, of narrow escapes from detention. Again, the woman was forced to beg the nuns to save her child, and yet again it was necessary for her to take him back to stop his pining. He was moved from convent to convent and finally, at the end of the war, he was transferred to an orphanage and later sent to Israel without his mother.

He had grown into a nervous, morose lad, suffering from chronic asthma. He had no companions and refused to make any. Embittered, lonely, tormented, Raphael could find no place for himself in the new land and eventually, hating everybody, he took to crime. On 21 August 1957 Raphael attempted to rob the Tsafon cinema in Tel Aviv. His plan did not succeed and the ticket-seller at the box office sounded the alarm. Raphael grew panicky and in his attempt to escape, he shot and killed the other.

Fidia Piattelli, the murdered man, was an Italian engineer who had married a German Protestant brought up in Italy.

During the war he had been interned by Mussolini's fascists but was later released thanks to his wife's intervention. In 1945, they both left for Israel. They had no children.

Raphael was arrested and brought to trial. He was convicted of murder and sentenced to life imprisonment. At the Ramla prison he seemed more morose and stranger than ever. He refused to associate with his fellow inmates, he was violent, troublesome and dangerous. He made various attempts to escape. Psychiatrists attributed his behaviour to his unfortunate childhood, his lack of a father and, more especially, to his early separation from his mother whom he had adored. Had she survived, all this might never have happened. Had she survived.

It was at this point that Heinke Piattelli, the wife of the murdered man, entered Raphael Blitz's life. She had been abroad at the time her husband died, and on her return she felt impelled to visit the prison and to meet the young rebel who had deprived her of her husband for the rest of her days. The first meeting passed in utter silence. She merely studied him as he eyed her with apprehension. In that silence a bond was created between them: a bond of mutual loss, of sympathy, of understanding.

Heinke Piattelli became a regular visitor to the prison. Being a violin teacher, she knew the value of music as a therapy to troubled minds and she brought Raphael a gift of a guitar. She taught and encouraged him to play. Before long, Raphael underwent a complete change in his behaviour. Not only did his love for music grow, but he developed an intense desire for study. He took a matriculation course and passed his finals in various subjects.

Eleven years passed since Heinke and Raphael first met and in that time his nature had entirely altered. Altered? Or returned to what it would have been had his childhood been normal and had he not been deprived of his mother at so tender an age? Perhaps in Heinke he found a substitute for her and perhaps in Raphael, Heinke found a son she longed to have and was unable to conceive? Was the bond which grew between them not a measure of that true love of man for his neighbour? That love which understands forgiveness and knows how to bring repose and dignity to a disturbed mind? I believe we have much to learn from Heinke Piattelli.

Raphael was eventually released from jail, has since married and started a family, and has become an honest, productive and respected citizen.

CS

Boys Town

'THE FIRST DAY they came, they set fire to a dog. The second day, they burnt a cat alive. The third day they attempted to burn down the school buildings. "Come now, boys," I told them, "we enjoy a bonfire as much as any of you, but let's have it out in the open where we can *all* join in." So the entire school gave up studying and we danced and sang religious songs round a huge bonfire in the fields.'

The man who was talking to me was Alexander Lynchner, Dean of the amazing ultra-modern campus in Jerusalem, known as Boys Town, where youngsters freely express their religious bent whilst studying academic and technical subjects. What Rabbi Lynchner had described to me was an experiment in admitting 30 sons of the dissident 'Black Panthers' – the under-privileged, poverty-stricken immigrants, mostly from the North African countries. After the event of the bonfire, those 30 boys spread the word and were joined by 120 more. Within four months, by being shown understanding, sympathy, and – above all – love, those boys were studying as seriously and as happily as their fellow pupils. And, what is more, they proved to be an excellent influence on their parents at home.

As is often the way with rebellious, unschooled youngsters, beneath their angry, chip-on-shoulder exteriors, lie intelligent, inquiring minds, bursting to cut through the rough outer crust and claim their rightful places in society: capable of forging ahead to become leaders, rulers, pacemakers of the nation.

The majority of the 1,250 students in Boys Town, Jerusalem have come from large families, many extremely poor and generally of Oriental origin. The founder, Alexander Lynchner believed strongly that it is possible in this space-rocket age to combine technical and scientific advancement with a love of God, and he offered the boys the opportunity to prove this. There are no fewer than four synagogue halls situated between the various classes in printing, offset and graphic design, carpentry, electronics science and humanities. At certain times of the day, the boys lay aside their slide-rules, their lathes and their tools, to pray as their fathers and grandfathers did before them.

Every piece of furniture, every shelf, bed, chair and table is made by the boys themselves: in the machine shop the lads built an 18-metre antenna commissioned by the Israel Broadcasting Service. In the electronics school I saw a new type of organ weighing only 10 lb which is capable of the full range of musical instruments, plus simulating the human voice. The organ was designed and built by a boy of 17.

Nothing remarkable or particularly unusual, some will say. If so, it is because I have failed to convey the most important aspect of all: the *happiness* which pervades the entire school. I have entered many churches, synagogues, mosques, academies and schools in my time, but nowhere have I encountered such contentment and joy as I found among the teachers and youngsters of Boys Town. No beating of the chest, no cringing beneath the weight of convention, no whispering of prayers in fear of an awesome

Goc of vengeance, but a full-throated joy in the love of boy for God and the knowledge that it is reciprocated.

The true definition of Rabbi is not just 'Master' but a teacher who learns *with* his pupils. This is exactly the approach I noticed at Boys Town. The teachers seemed to be joking, cajoling, teasing, encouraging their pupils to find the maximum fun in the lesson – not merely to cram knowledge into their skulls but, above all else, to *enjoy* learning. And that is the impression I will most remember of Boys Town, Jerusalem: the delight and the fun these youngsters derive from religion and from studying at a school which marries the 'faith of the past with the skills of today'.

$$\text{\Large{CB}}$$

If Only ...

I MET HIM ON a kibbutz. His name was Itai and he was five years old. Not tall for his age, fair, tousled hair and pale blue eyes. To get him to talk to me at all – let alone run the full gamut of his knowledge of English – was something of a triumph. To him, I was an outsider: a stranger who had no business keeping my guide, Haggai (who was his daddy), away from him for so long!

When I first saw Itai he was playing on the sandy soil with his young companions. Playing, but not smiling. With them, yet strangely aloof. As Haggai greeted him, he glanced up at the familiar face and quickly looked away again, ignoring Haggai's presence. I had seen my youngest child do this to me on my return from abroad: a sort of punishment for having been absent for a week or more. I waited, confidently, for I recognized the game and I knew the next move. It was not long coming. Suddenly, Itai rose, opened his arms to

Haggai and waited to be swung into the air. Man and boy did not kiss each other as father and little son are wont to do: instead Itai gripped his legs around Haggai's middle, placed is arms round the other's neck, and snuggled his head against Haggai's chest. This gesture of affection over, Itai jumped down, took Haggai's hand and pulled him away from me towards the beach. When he saw that I was following, he began to run, dragging Haggai as though he wanted to forge ahead too fast for me to catch up. Only once did his eyes meet mine, and the hostility troubled me.

 Luckily I know a trump card which doesn't often fail. I ignored Itai and began slowly and quietly to clown with my tape recorder, giving it a 'life of its own': letting it talk back at me, hit me on the head, appear to spin me round in circles and finally force me to somersault and land on my behind in the soft sand. I sneaked a glance at the boy and knew at once that the thaw had begun. I did some more clowning and quite suddenly Itai came close to me and said in Hebrew: 'Come and see my cave.' He showed no pleasure but, when he took my hand in his free one (the other hand had not let go of Haggai since their first moment of contact), I knew I had been accepted.

Have you ever known the thrill of a child's approval after a hostile beginning? I hope so, for it is difficult to describe. It is something like seeing the sunset over a calm sea after the storm, or the awakening day express itself in pastel shades in a clear sky. Haggai told the lad I had four children of my own. Itai searched my face with his large serious eyes, then began to gather shells in the sand as a gift from him to them, to 'the children of the clown'.

On the way back we met Itai's mother. I found it strange that she and Haggai did not embrace, but merely shook hands and exchanged a greeting. 'Shalom, Haggai.' 'Shalom, Hani.' They spoke in Hebrew and Itai left me to hold both their hands in his. Then he led us all to the library to show me his classroom and sleeping quarters. There his friends were seated in a circle, listening to their teacher telling them a story. As soon as they heard I was a foreigner, they broke into a 'foreign song'. (No matter that 'Frère Jacques' was French. I was from 'abroad' and they knew a song 'from abroad'.)

I felt the need to reciprocate in some way, so I did some more clowning, but I could not succeed in bringing a smile to the lips of one of the most beautiful children I have ever seen: a very dark Indian girl with huge eyes and brilliant white teeth. 'Another problem child,' I told myself and glanced at Itai who seemed proud of his new possession, this English jester who turned on his clowning act at the sound of song or a laugh from his companions. Itai grasped my hand and led me away from the group towards a small building set apart from the rest. In it were 22 framed photographs of young men, perhaps between 18 and 21, and two of older men, I would say around 30 to 35. Itai took one from the lower shelf and held it out to me. 'Abba,' he said. 'My daddy' I glanced at Haggai who nodded and later filled in the gap for me.

'I'm only his adopted father,' he said. 'It's a common enough story here in Israel. You see, I was a member of this kibbutz and Itai's father, Aaron, was my best friend. He was a great one with the girls and when the kibbutz sent him to the city to study at university, Hani followed him and insisted on sharing his flat and caring for him. She knew Aaron would never marry her – but she loved him and that was enough for her. Suddenly, she came back to the kibbutz, and eight months later Aaron visited us. He saw that Hani was big with child – his child. You see, Hani had left him when she realized she was pregnant because she didn't want to be a burden to Aaron. When he learned this, he disappeared for two whole days to think things over. Then he came back and asked Hani to be his wife.

'Three hundred guests were at the wedding, for Aaron was very popular; and we danced and sang throughout most of the night. Then the war came and the young men were called immediately. Both Aaron and I were paratroopers. I was lucky. I came back. Aaron did not. So Itai was born without ever having seen his father – and I became his guardian. I come to see him as often as I can and he treats me like his real father ... but I can never make him laugh. Thank you for clowning. You almost made him smile. He's a serious boy – unlike his father – and he has his own way of working things out. When he was two-and-a-half, I took him to see an airforce display and when he saw the parachutists coming down the sky he asked me: "D'you know what those round things are up there?" "They're clouds, Itai," I said. "Oh no, they're not. You see, the parachutists are angry because my daddy isn't there to jump with them ... so they've burnt holes in the sky."'

I asked Itai if there was anything I could send him from London and he replied: 'Yes, foreign stamps.' A modest enough request from a serious boy of five who goes each day to the House of Remembrance to say 'hello' to the photograph of his daddy. His daddy who he has never met, and who would in all probability be playing with him right now: leap-frogging on the sand, exploring the caves, teaching him about the fish and the sea, tucking him in at night and telling him a bedtime story, sharing the best years of his childhood, perhaps even gifting Itai with a brother. If only .. If only ...

☙

Let There Be No Dew

OVERLOOKING THE lake of Galilee in Israeli is a large kibbutz known for its hospitality to foreign visitors. I stood on the balcony of the dining hall and gazed across the lake to the mountains of Gilboa on the Syrian side of the trouble-ridden border. There, three gently inclining mountains rise to immense heights, overlooking the surrounding countryside like nature's sentinels, placed there to remind us how ant-like are men's struggles for the space between two blades of grass. Vegetation appears to be rich on the mountain slopes, with the exception of the centre one, where it ceases in a marked semicircle of utter barrenness near the top – a sad brown patch against the yellows and greens.

I remarked on this strange fact to an elderly member of the kibbutz who had stepped out onto the balcony. 'Why do you find it strange?' he replied. 'Don't you know your Bible?'

I thought back to the events I could recall for which this area was famous. The wars between the ancient Israelites and their neighbours, David's struggle against King Saul. Ah, David: a glimmer of understanding came into my mind.

'Wasn't that where Saul and David fought?' I asked.

'Getting warm, my friend. Where Saul and the Philistines fought. Jonathan was killed and Saul was wounded. And when he found he'd lost his son and lost the battle, he killed himself.'

'So Saul and Jonathan died on that very mountain,' I mused. 'But surely that in itself could not have made the land barren?'

'My friend, your Bible history is neglected. Have you forgotten how David cursed the spot?'

For the moment I could not think what the Israeli meant. Then it came to me. When David heard of the death of Saul and Jonathan, he composed one of the most moving laments ever to be uttered; and in it, he willed barrenness on the mountain. He said,

> *Let there be no dew, neither let there be rain upon you nor*
> *fields of offerings*
> *For there the shield of the mighty is vilely cast away,*
> *The shield of Saul, as though he had not been anointed with*
> *oil.*

I am not superstitious and I don't believe in curses and yet, when I think that in the 3,000 years since the day David called upon the rain not to fall upon Gilboa, nor the fields to grow full with their offerings, the spot where Saul and Jonathan died has nurtured no new life, I cannot help wondering. Could it be that man's ears were not alone in hearing and being moved by David's sorrow on that bitter day of battle?

CB

A Handful of Toffees

SHE LOOKED SO frail as she came out of the shop in Mea Shearim, in Jerusalem, holding an alarm clock in one hand and grasping the doorpost with the other. I tried not to let her notice my curiosity as she carefully guided her steps on the uneven pavement which was in the course of being repaired. I offered her my arm for support for it was dangerous for a woman as old as she to negotiate the broken stones.

The paving slabs became more regular just before the corner and she let go my arm with a quiet 'toda raba' (thank you very much). I turned away and took several paces forward, but I glanced back at her when I saw the traffic-lights ahead and wondered whether she would turn right or want to cross the main road. Again I took her arm and I noticed that she continued to walk as carefully as though she were still treading on broken ground. I asked her if she wanted to cross the road, but her reply left me no wiser for she answered in Hebrew. I tried Italian but she shook her head. 'Non, non … je ne parle pas l'Italien malheureusement, jeune homme!' I was pleased that, after-all, we could converse in a common tongue. We turned the corner and only a few yards further on, she held me back as she crossed in front of me and pushed open a pair of narrow broken old doors. She led me into a dark corridor with room only to walk in single file. A few more paces and she placed her foot on the first of the stone steps rising ahead to the next floor.

I bade her 'adieu', but she would not let go my hand. 'Non, non … venez avec moi … je vous en prie.' I was surprised to see that she climbed the steps one foot ahead of the other with a sudden vigour which she had not displayed in the street. I suppose the familiarity of home ground brought back her confidence. At the top, she removed a key from her handbag and unlocked the door. Again she grasped my hand firmly and drew me into the room. Then she locked the door behind us. This immediately worried me for I did not like the idea of being locked in the room with an elderly stranger, and I found myself growing tense. She must have sensed this, for she smiled at me and murmured: 'N'avez pas peur, jeune homme … je ne vous ferais pas du mal!'

I had to chuckle at the thought of this tiny old soul, so close to her grave, doing me harm, and my quiet laugh put her at ease. She still had not let go my hand as she deposited the alarm clock on a small table, opened a wardrobe door and took out a biscuit tin, flipped open the hinged lid with her thumb in an expert manner, and then released my hand in order to dip hers in the tin and grasp a fistful of toffees which she thrust into my palm, accepting no refusal. Then she offered to make me a glass of camomile tea. I declined and explained I must be on my way, but she did not accept this. 'Asseyez-vous … je vais vous demander un conseil.'

She seemed so determined, there was nothing for it but to obey. I sat on the edge of the bed and looked around me. The room was almost as narrow as the staircase, and contained only the bed, the little table and a wardrobe which must once have been an attractive piece of furniture. The evidence pointed to poverty, but the spotlessly clean bedcover and the well-washed walls impressed me. A faded curtain enclosed a little gas cooker and a few shelves with utensils and crockery. As the old lady busied herself preparing the camomile, there was a knock at a door I had not previously noticed at the end of the room just behind the head of the bed.

The old lady glanced up quickly at me and I could see that her eyes had grown nervous behind her thick glasses. She gave me a penetrating stare which seemed to pierce deep into my being. When it was obvious that I too had heard the knock, she edged past me and unlocked the door.

'Je sense que je peus compter sur votre discretion, Monsieur. Viens, mon petit … n'ai pas peur … c'est un jeune homme qui a du coeur. Il ne te fera pas du mal. Viens … viens … Yeheskele.'

She put her hand through the doorway and drew into the room a strange little being. As he came out of the shadow, I couldn't avoid gasping. Before me stood a handicapped boy with the body of a child but the head of an old man. His eyes could not focus well and his head moved as though it were not firmly attached to his neck. I tried hard not to show my reaction, but the woman was too quick for me.

'Don't show pity for him, Monsieur. His mind is handicapped, but he's probably happier than you.' Her English was good and I was taken aback. Why had she not answered me in English in the street when I first spoke to her? I hadn't time to voice my question for she led the boy to the bed and sat him by me, talking to him the while in Hebrew in the gentlest of tones. When he was comfortable, she carried on preparing the herbal tea while she spoke to me.

'You must forgive my dreadful English, but I must try to talk in a language he doesn't understand for I wouldn't want him to be hurt by anything I say. People think he is silly in the head because of the way he looks, but you'd be amazed at the struggle to express himself which lies behind that crippled mind. Yeheskel understands almost everything I say in

Hebrew, French and Arabic, and he has such love and gentleness in his soul that he deserves our understanding. I think the Almighty withdrew speech from him because if he could speak, his wisdom would make us blush.

'Prends ça, prends ça, mon petit agneau ...' she murmured to the boy as she spoonfed him from a cup of milk.

'Do you see how he drinks without spilling a drop? He's a good boy and I love him dearly. It is dangerous for me to show him to a stranger, but you have shown much kindness and I sense you will understand my problem and not give me away.' Give her away? I was truly intrigued now, and my writer's mind tuned in its memory computer as I sensed a good story.

She stared deeply into my eyes for a long moment, then she took a breath, sighed, and began: 'He is my grandson: my daughter's boy. We came from Baghdad, from Iraq, when the Jews had to escape 20 years ago. We came here and started our life again. My son-in-law would not leave me behind even though he had 11 children and a wife as well as his own mother to support. Oh he was such a good man. I couldn't have wished for a better husband for my daughter. I have trust in my God, but I will never understand why He should want to take a good man and his family – such strong, sturdy children – and leave only this useless old remnant and a boy who cannot help himself! But His ways are His ways and there must be a reason we are perhaps not permitted to know in this world. Do you believe in a world to come? Of course you must, for I see from your skullcap you are religious. I do – and I know one thing for certain. My Yeheskel has a free passport to that piece of heaven reserved for the truly good. I pray he will put in a word for me, in spite of my impatience and inadequacy. C'est vrais, n'est-ce pas, mon petit chou?'

She pulled the boy's head against her breast and gently stroked his tousled hair as she continued. 'My son-in-law did not earn very much – he was a clerk in a government office and his salary was hardly enough to keep us all – which is why I refused to be a burden to him and I rented this little room. I do well enough, you know. I make repairs to people's clothes ... and sometimes, God willing, I get some lace curtains to make or even a wedding veil ... and I manage. My grandchildren often came to visit me and that is why I keep a tin of sweets in my wardrobe always handy, and I have no grandchildren left to give them to. My little Yeheskel doesn't like sweet things. N'est-ce pas, mon âme?'

She hugged the boy almost fiercely, and it was not difficult to sense the tragic longing beneath her gesture. 'He is all I have left in the world, and I love him more than myself. If I were to lose him too ... life would not be worth living (God should forgive me)!'

I was touched to realize how a woman who looked close to 90, clung to life with such tenacity and I wished I had had a tape recorder to capture the vigour of her voice and personality – but I never seem to have one with me at such golden moments.

'What happened to his parents?' I asked. Her eyes clouded over and she was silent for a long moment.

'You know we have bomb incidents frequently, when young men with a distorted sense of values revenge themselves on innocent victims for the wrongs they feel were done to their own people in the past. You may have read in the newspapers about a bus which was blown up by a parcel bomb left on the luggage rack. Twenty-seven people were on the bus and only a few survived. All Yeheskel's family, his father, mother, his ten brothers and sisters – all were on that bus – and not one of them survived. Yeheskel had been left with me while the family went on a short holiday to the seaside. The first holiday they have had since they came to Israel. I read and hear myself of such killings, but this sort of thing happens to others – never to your own family. But this time, the Angel of Death found my son-in-law's name inscribed in the book of life and closed the page too soon.

And all I have left is this young son of my daughter, whose mind is locked in a body which cannot synchronize with his brain and nerves, and who will always need someone else to be his eyes and tongue.

'I was so afraid the authorities would consider me too old to take care of him that I decided to hide him here and pretend he had gone to his Maker together with the rest of the family. If they find him, they'll dismiss him as unimportant and they will put him in an institution, and I know he would never be happy there. They are so busy, how could they ever have time and patience to understand his needs and give him back even a little of the love he offers to others without expecting anything in return? He is no trouble, you know; he eats seldom and he never asks more attention than you can give him. God gifts those who are unfortunate with a quality others do not possess … and his gift is that he always senses your mood and can somehow manage to comfort you when you are sad and to give you warmth and sympathy when you most need them. I am full of years and ought to have gone long ago. I know now that God kept me alive to care for this boy, and I am grateful for the duty He has granted me. But I do not know how much time I have left … after all, I have no contract with God. What will happen to him when my turn comes?'

She stopped talking and looked directly at me with such appeal in her eyes that I knew what would come next and I felt ashamed at my instinctive reaction.

'I judge all men by their eyes, and yours tell me you are a person I can truly trust, or I would not be telling you my secret. Now I am going to ask you something very important. Something prompted you to offer me your arm in the street when I was nervous of the broken pavement. Maybe that something was the hand of God who sent you to me this day. Perhaps He was showing me that you are the one to take over when I am gone? Will you, kind sir, take this boy and care for him? I can tell you are a family man … I expect you have children of your own. Each new child brings his own luck and his own reward for your care. Please, please take Yeheskel with your own sons ... and you will never ever regret it, I promise you. These handicapped children are closer to God than many others of His beings, and they create an aura of His goodness which sends out radiations of strength and joy to all who come in contact with them. It is the very gift of life I am offering you – do you not see that? Please, please, do accept ...'

She came very close to me and took my hand between hers. I could sense the pace of her heart beating faster than normal and the amazing strength of her grip was almost painful. I felt like a murderer as a voice I did not recognize as my own seemed to come from my throat.

'No ... No ... I'm so very sorry ... but that would not be possible. I'm returning to England in two days and without the authorities' permission I'd be stopped at the airport. They might think I had kidnapped your grandson. They'd never let him go with me. Do you understand, Madame? I'm very sorry ... but it just wouldn't be possible. Believe me, he'd be better off in an institution where they'd take proper care of him. They have very good homes for these boys, really they have.' To my shame, I was so taken aback by the impossibility of her suggestion that I found myself at the door, trying to get out of the room before I remembered that the old lady had locked it. She turned the key, then opened the door for me.

'Shalom, Monsieur. Thank you for your patience in listening to me. I understand your concern. Please, I implore you, do not give me away. I will find someone to take care of Yeheskel. It is clear God did not mean him to be you. Shalom, Shalom, Monsieur.'

A moment later I was in the street, walking towards my hotel.

I have thought so much about it since then. Did I really meet that old lady? Somehow I can't believe it and yet ... I still have those toffees she thrust into my hand: those toffees which are always on my conscience. Was I right to keep her secret?

CB

Between Two Blades of Grass

'HISTORY REPEATS itself!' How often do we hear that phrase? And how often does it prove true?! Here is an example.

During the 1914–18 war, a young English major serving in Lord Allenby's army in Palestine had been given orders to attack a Turkish stronghold which had so far proved impregnable. Now, it is one thing calmly to issue orders which are typed by efficient secretaries and sent through efficient channels to a destination many hundreds of miles away, but place yourself for a moment in the shoes of the brigade major who receives those orders and who discovers that all previous attacks have not only failed, but of 1,000 officers and men who took part in them, only 187 returned alive: 813 men dead, in order to challenge ownership of the space between two blades of grass! The Turks were entrenched in a village which stood on a rocky prominence on the other side of a deep valley. The major studied the limited methods of penetration, and each and every one spelt but one word: suicide. But, in the army, orders are orders!

He thought again of the name of the village occupied by the Turks. It was called Michmash, and it seemed somehow familiar. He turned the wheels of memory until the cogs engaged. He had heard it during one of the evening Bible readings with his Welsh grandmother. But what had

69

happened there worthy of being recorded for all time? He searched his Bible and eventually he found it, in the Book of Samuel. He read there, 'And Saul and Jonathan, his son and the people that were present with them, abode in G beah of Benjamin, but the Philistines encamped in Michmash.' It then went on to tell how Jonathan and his armour-bearers crossed over during the night to the Philistines' garrison on the other side, and how they passed between two sharp rocks named Bozez and Seneh. They clambered up the cliff and overpowered the garrison, as the Bible says, 'within as it were an half acre of land, which a yoke of oxen might plough'. The main body of the enemy, awakened by the noise, thought they were surrounded by Saul's troops and 'melted away', and they went on beating down one another. Thereupon Saul attacked with his whole force and beat the enemy.

The young major wondered whether the narrow pass through the rocks still existed, and at the end of it the 'half acre of land'. He called his fellow officers and they read through the passage together. Patrols were sent out during the night. They found the pass which was thinly held by Turks and which led past two jagged rocks – obviously Bozez and Seneh. On top, beside the village of Michmash, they could see by the light of the moon a small flat field.

The young major decided. 'Saul and Jonathan were great soldiers … they've shown me the way.' And he altered his plan of attack. Instead of deploying the whole brigade, he sent one company only through the pass under cover of darkness. The few Turks whom they met were overpowered without a sound, the cliffs were scaled, and shortly before daybreak the company had taken up a position on the 'half acre of land'.

The main army of the Turks woke up and took to their heels in disorder since they thought they were being surrounded by Allenby's army, just as – centuries earlier – the Philistines in the exact same position, had thought *they* were surrounded by the entire army of Saul, and not just a handful of men. Within a matter of hours, the brigade major was able to inform headquarters: 'Enemy routed. Position taken. No casualties.'

That night, as he destroyed the farewell letter to his wife the major blessed his Welsh grandmother and the inspiration which caused him to turn the pages of history back thousands of years to learn a lesson in the art of war – without slaughter – from Saul and Jonathan.

ॐ

The Fringe of Eternity

THREE OF MY children, my eldest son Jonathan and my twin daughters, had been studying in Jerusalem for two years, and my work had taken me there for ten days of research and recordings. When I finished my assignment, I was given the loan of an empty flat for my last weekend so that I could spend it with my youngsters.

On Friday afternoon, Jonathan arrived laden with food for Sabbath, and set immediately to cleaning the entire flat, dusting, scrubbing, making the place feel cared for. The girls prepared the food, lit the candles, and welcomed the Sabbath like a bride.

There was silence in the flat, a silence disturbed by realization. The realization that your little ones are now adults: able to make their own decisions, to forge their own path, and are no longer dependent on their father for anything but the wherewithal to buy the few necessities of life. It comes as something of a shock to all parents but, combating that shock comes the pride and pleasure in observing them: the decisiveness of the lad, the charm of the girls as they cross the room with the ease and grace of an unhurrying wind.

There's another pleasure, too – the pleasure of *listening* to the 'builders' of the future, listening to *your* builders. Not talking *to* them, or laying down the fatherly law, but opening your ears to the 'wisdom' of the young, sharing *their* concerns, *their* desires, *their* hopes.

After our Sabbath meal, while the girls cleared the things, Jonathan and I stepped out onto the balcony and stood looking across the valley to the moonlit heights beyond. Those heights which had buried so many opponents: the Israelites, the Assyrians, King Herod, the Roman Emperors, the Persians and the Turks. Now the plains were resplendent with new green growth and 'shalom' – peace – seemed to radiate its contentment as far as the eye could see.

No words passed between my son and me. They were not needed. The centuries which stretched behind seemed very present, and I could no longer tell whether I was in this era, or one which had disappeared long since. Ahead of me, around me, were the ghosts of lives which had completed their span so that I could take up the mantle, and, in turn, pass it on in an eternal relay. They were part of me, and I was part of them: a connecting link between those who were banished from their homeland to linger in exile, to those who faced the Spanish Inquisition, the Russian pogroms, Hitler's maniacal holocaust, and the flesh and spirit which went to make up this particular Jew.

Slowly, a sense of well-being, of calm and of belonging came over me – the sense of having returned home. I was aware of a 'presence' I could only sense: a oneness of earth, heavens, stars, desert – my grown son beside me and the other flesh of my flesh in the room behind me … In that moment I sensed the fringe of eternity.

Part III

His Mysterious Ways

There for the Asking

I ONCE HEARD a lecture by a Swedish doctor, a Dr Brunler, who maintained that everything alive gives off radiations, and that any object with which these radiations come into contact, retains them for all eternity. At the time I thought this theory was far-fetched, but the longer I live, the more I find myself wondering.

If Dr Brunler was correct there is not a house or wall or piece of furniture which is not reflecting these radiations, enveloping us with echoes of the past. I can't help feeling that our subconscious is aware of this, even if we are not. I am certain too that our moods, our behaviour, our very thoughts are influenced by these radiations, whether to the good, or perhaps even to evil.

Have you never entered a strange room or house, and sensed the atmosphere of the place: known somehow whether there has been joy or tragedy previously in the home? Have you not felt strangely uneasy? By the same token, sensitive people who walk on the hills and the mountains where great events have once taken place, will be encircled by the radiations attached to them by the giants of history. Can they perhaps be trying to tell us something – to warn us – or admonish us? And can it be that if only our mental receivers were tuned in accurately, we would understand the message and act accordingly? Could we avert catastrophe, change the course of events, if only we were on the right wavelength to recognize the radiations which encompass us?

And what of the inanimate objects which have also received the radiations? We assume that they have no life of their own: but are we perhaps concluding this from our all too narrow human conception? Doesn't the Hebrew Talmud – that monumental commentary on the Torah – refer to mountains 'dancing for joy', and actually vying with each other for the honour of receiving God's Law? Doesn't the psalmist refer to plants singing their praise of the Almighty? A little fanciful, would you say? And yet, recently the BBC broadcast an interview with the inventor of a machine which actually recorded the sounds made by plants, and the voices of crocuses were a revelation: one could hear a genuine tune sung by scores of tiny childlike voices in quivering delight. If only the human ear could be so gifted!

Could it perhaps be that our subconscious possesses this ability but that few of us are aware of it, or able to penetrate the mystery? I remember my dear father, rest his soul, used to say: '*use* your subconscious, Robert – it possesses infinite knowledge and it's there for the asking … yet you neglect it!'

Do you know, the first prayer a religious Jew utters on waking up is to thank the Almighty for returning to him his soul. Does that not imply that the soul takes off during sleep, perhaps to climb into the realms of the unknown, perhaps to sit with the angels, even to hear the very voice of God? Could it be that deep in our subconscious is the awareness of this? And that our soul is trying to communicate it to our minds?

God of our Fathers, grant us the ability to tap that source of all knowledge, all understanding and all love.

CB

A Tale of Two Legs

H ER NAME WAS Charyn, a handsome girl of 19 with a pleasant disposition and much charm. She hailed from Brooklyn, New York, but I met her in Jerusalem where she had come in search of her roots and an identity. Her story was similar to so many I had heard before. Parents whose Jewishness was to them merely accidental and little to be expressed, brought up with scant knowledge of her heritage and no pride in her religion.

Charyn was athletic and enjoyed the current craze for jogging. Early each morning, before breakfast, she would don her tracksuit and shoes, tie her hair tidily in a bun and take a long trot around the block near her home.

Without notice, one morning she found the ease and grace of her movements had frozen into stiffness in the muscles of her left leg. After a few days, the effort to jog became painful and the doctor was sent for. He diagnosed strain and advised her to rest. Charyn was confined to her bed with enforced inactivity and pain. Later the doctor called again and became concerned. He had detected a blood clot and wanted her removed immediately to hospital. Charyn refused because that day happened to be Yom Kippur and she would not travel. The doctor was taken aback. He knew the family well and was aware of their lack of religious observance. What had happened to bring about this sudden change in attitude?

What he did not know was that a friend of Charyn had visited her during the week and had lent her a book to read which was no more than a child's guide to Judaism. Something within her had stirred the dormant genes of those past generations whose faith had withstood the savagery of the Russian pogroms and enforced conversion and were now whispering strange messages through her bloodstream. The Day of Atonement acquired a new meaning to Charyn, and without really understanding why, she found an unusual obstinacy dictating her refusal to be transported to hospital.

'But you could be in danger, my girl. I hate to tell you this, but I am very disturbed by your condition and it's important that we take X-rays of your leg before making what could be a drastic decision. I cannot accept responsibility for what could happen to you if you refuse.'

Charyn's parents were out of town and there was no one else to persuade or advise her. The doctor sent for help and literally forced the girl into an ambulance and drove her off to hospital. There, the doctor's fears were confirmed and preparations made to amputate the leg in order to save her life. But first it would be necessary to inject a dye into the veins and X-ray the leg to check the extent of the damage.

'It's Yom Kippur and I will not allow you,' was all Charyn would say. For several hours, the nurses and doctors argued with her – to no avail. Unable to contact her parents, the surgeon took the responsibility of final decision: amputation. Charyn fought like a wild animal, possessed of an inner strength she never suspected existed, and determined at all cost that no knife would be used on her this precious day.

It was at this point that fate intervened. A surgeon of higher authority happened to be in the hospital, he was consulted and he examined Charyn's leg. He was impressed by the strength of her refusal and was not altogether convinced of the need to amputate. 'We'll give it another day,' he proclaimed.

The day became a week, became a month, and Charyn walked out of that hospital in possession of both her legs and a new faith germinating within. She asked to go to Jerusalem where she joined my twin daughters in the Seminar and found peace of mind and happiness. Her parents emulated her example and are now observant Jews.

But that is only part of the story. Act two occurred a year later. Charyn received news that her brother had developed a serious infection in his leg and the doctors had decided to amputate. History repeats itself. On Yom Kippur, Charyn attended Synagogue service in Jerusalem and said to Hashem: 'Please, punish me instead; but save my brother's leg, I beg of you.'

At the end of the service, on her way out, Charyn slipped, fell down the stone steps and hurt her leg. A young man had entered the Synagogue just then and came to her assistance.

'Charyn, I'm glad I found you. I've good news for you. I know you were concerned about your brother and I just telephoned your parents. They told me he's going to be all right. They don't need to amputate!'

Coincidence? Or, yet another example of His mysterious ways?

ശ

Accept My Health

THIS IS NOT AN easy tale to recount – it is even more difficult to believe. If the girls in question were not my own twin daughters, I for one would find it far-fetched. But then, 'There are more things in heaven and earth ...'

When they were little, the twins developed a language of their own for private communication, and no one could enter their little wonderworld unless invited. Liana was fearless and Anya was afraid of being afraid. When they received their innoculation against smallpox before visiting Israel, Liana felt no pain, and proudly displayed the plaster on her arm to her sister. As the doctor approached Anya with the needle, she winced with pain even though it had not yet touched her. Liana fainted flat out, seeing her sister cry.

Another time they were both in the bath and my wife asked me to take them out and dry them while she prepared dinner. I placed Liana on the mat and bent down to pick up Anya. As I did so, she slipped under the water, but my hands had already reached her and I drew her out without a gurgle or gasp. I remember thinking at the time that the incident was more balletic than dangerous. I turned round to find Liana had fainted at the sight of her sister – as she thought – drowning.

They were 16 when Anya went to America to a seminar and Liana – at home in London – suddenly developed glandular fever. She was really quite ill. We decided not to inform Anya, but she wrote to us to say that she had been feeling unwell and had visited two doctors. The first could find nothing wrong and the second said she appeared to display the symptoms of glandular fever, but did not have glandular fever!

On another occasion, Liana caught a mysterious virus which sapped her strength and made her weaker each day. Medicines had little effect and she seemed to be getting worse. At night she would develop a high temperature and toss about feverishly in bed, her nightdress soaked with perspiration.

Anya came up with the theory that, if the affinity between them was so great that she could suffer a phantom illness in sympathy with her sick twin, perhaps it was equally possible to convey *good* health to the other. Anya said her morning and evening prayers regularly, and that night I heard her whispering: 'Now listen, Shwesti ... I'm fighting fit at the moment and, with Hashem's permission, I want to share my good health with you. So my health is going to fight your virus and I want you to send it packing!'

Would you believe that the morning after, Liana awoke very late after the first restful night in over a week, and promptly demanded a hearty breakfast, although the very sight of food had previously made her nauseous. I asked Anya if she had had anything to do with it. 'Well ...,' she replied, 'in my mind, I just told Liana to accept my health, because I didn't want to catch her illness. And I suppose the positive worked just as well as the negative.'

The positive! On the face of it Liana's rapid recovery was pure coincidence: and yet, could it be that her twin had hit on some source of spiritual energy we might all possess, but do not know how to tap? Can one really, through the strength of love, inject one's own state of health into another being? The Talmud tells of healing by the laying on of hands. Shouldn't the laying on of the mind prove even more efficacious? I have a feeling that Anya's theory is worth exploiting further. 'After all,' I ask myself, 'did not the All Perfect One make the seemingly impossible possible when he created us in His own image?' Could it be that a Third Party acted as the 'conductor' between my daughters? Who knows!

 C3

To Tina – A Son

'MR RIETTI, I'm afraid I must ask you to leave the room.' It was the surgeon speaking to me as he bent over my wife who lay in the delivery room awaiting the birth of our fourth child. Till that moment everything had gone smoothly. Tina's labour had started at the expected time, she had not been in undue pain, I had been permitted to remain by her side, and I looked forward to the thrill of actually seeing my baby emerge into this world.

Then, suddenly, Tina emitted a low moan quite different from the quick breathing sounds I had become accustomed to. She tossed her head from side to side and her nails made their imprint in the flesh of my palm. At that moment the surgeon returned, his huge rubber wellingtons slip-slopping along the floor. He bent down to examine Tina and, without straightening up, gave that sudden order to me to leave the room. As I did so, the nurse was already giving Tina an injection to send her to sleep and the doctor drew a fresh pair of gloves over his hands in preparation for – what?

I sat in the waiting-room and closed my eyes. My mind took me back to the time, two years before, when we had decided we would like to have another child, and three different gynaecologists had warned us that it was unlikely Tina would be able to conceive again, and, should she do so, the chances of her fulfilling her time were remote.

Well, despite the warning, despite our own belief that it was no longer possible, one morning Tina announced to me with the certainty of female instinct, that our twin daughters would no longer be our youngest. The pregnancy had been tough and Tina had had to take great care. But the dangerous landmarks had all passed and we seemed within minutes of that great event when, clearly, complications had arisen and the surgeon did not want me present.

For three-quarters of an hour, I sat in the waiting-room. I did not know then that my baby had twisted himself round in the womb, and – much more serious – the umbilical cord had tightened around his neck and was in the process of strangling him. I did not know, but the bond between Tina and myself was such that I sensed the struggle going on within her: the struggle to *give* new life and not to kill, nor to die.

I thought of our 12 years of life together, of the fun we had had. I thought of those stupid, mundane moments which can break a marriage: the endless cooking, washing and ironing, the tiredness, the lack of help, the children's quarrels and screams. I recalled that I seemed always to be abroad filming when the crises arose and Tina had to cope alone: like the time my son almost crushed his finger, or when my little girl broke three fingers in a fall at school. I thought of her patience with my shortcomings, and of the sacrifices the wife of any actor is called on to make. And suddenly I was frightened. Very, very frightened.

My mind searched for the means of communicating comfort to her. At first the words would not come, so I took refuge in traditional prayer: '... and when I passed by thee and saw thee weltering in thine own blood, I said unto thee: "in thy blood, live"; yea, I said unto thee: "in thy blood, live".'

At last the surgeon came in and told me it had been a very near thing, but now all was well and I could go in and see Tina and the babe. I looked at my lovely Tina, unconscious and unsightly in her exhausted state. She had lost a great deal of blood, but she was over the worst. Close by, in a metal cot, lay our newborn son, Benjamin, the marks from the forceps visible on his temples. In that moment I decided to name him Chaim after his grandfather. 'Chaim' – which means life. For, in that moment, as perhaps never before, I realized how good it was to be alive.

∝   ∝   ∝

After this talk was broadcast, the following review by Jeremy Rundall appeared in *The Sunday Times* for that week:

> A relief then, to find a tiny five minute flame on Thursday's *Thought for the Day*. On the week's theme of 'Good to be Alive' Robert Rietti alone conveyed immediately and brilliantly a personal experience – the difficult birth of his and Tina's latest one. OK, so Rietti is a professional actor. Yet the others before were public men too, and they spoke mainly in cliches. But to hear how Benjamin, wrongly set in his mother's womb and half-strangled, appeared after a climactic two hours alive and kicking, was to feel brushed by the Almighty. Which is what these programmes are supposed to be about.

Birth Dates

AFTER THE BIRTH of our twins, the surgeon had warned us that it was dangerous for my wife Tina to have any more children. She would like to have had eight, but she took the news philosophically and we were grateful for the three with which we had been blessed. My firstborn, Jonathan, had other ideas, however, and night after night, in his prayers, he entreated the Almighty to grant him a baby brother. Two girls ganging up on him were just too much for any boy!

One morning we awoke to the fact that another little pair of feet were on the way, and, despite the surgeon's warning, Tina was determined this one would emerge into the world safe and sound, at no matter what cost to her own health. In due course, the day of her labour was upon her and she lay in the hospital bed, scared in case the newborn proved to be a girl, for she knew that would break Jonathan's heart! Her time came and a new pair of lungs protested lustily against the surgeon's traditional slap on the bare bottom. The nurse whispered in Tina's ear, 'It's a boy.'

All was apparently well with Jonathan, but we did not know that his happiness was not complete. Eleven years later, during a preparatory lesson for his bar mitzvah, he confessed to his Rabbi that he had held a secret sorrow in his heart all this time, a sorrow which had been caused by God.

'What had He to do with it?' asked the Rabbi.

'Because my twin sisters were born on my father's birthday, and I prayed to Hashem, not only for a brother but that he should be born on *my* birthday. Mummy might have made it, but the surgeon didn't want to postpone his holiday, and he "induced" my baby brother to come four days earlier!'

'Well now ...' said Rabbi Levy. 'Let's take a look at the Hebrew calendar.' Believe it or not, Benjamin had been born on Jonathan's Hebrew birth date!

'But then ...' as an afterthought, Jonathan exclaimed, 'so if my sisters were born on Daddy's English birth date, that isn't so important after all!'

But Rabbi Levy was not easily daunted. 'What year were they born? Well, let's see what the Jewish calendar has to say about that.'

Have you guessed? That very year, the Hebrew and English calendars happened to coincide, so my twin daughters shared the best of both worlds! Coincidence, or design? Only He knows!

CR

Take From My Years

ACCORDING TO THE Bible, the ancient prophets were able to converse with God and even to 'strike a pact' with Him. I know of one ordinary mortal who attempted this very thing in Iraq, not so many years ago.

My wife's father, Semah, was a wealthy young pharmacist at the age of 26. One day, while walking through one of the countless narrow alleys in Baghdad, he noticed a pretty girl glancing out of her window. Her age? Perhaps nine, certainly not more. 'That girl will be my bride,' he said to himself, and that same day a proposal was made to the girl's mother. Her father, Moshi, was away in Egypt and her mother took it upon herself to accept. On his return, the poor man received the news in anger. His only daughter, a bride-to-be before ten summers had been granted her? Never! Moshi took the girl, whose name was Habibah, and drove away from Baghdad in a caravan.

Young Semah saddled his horse and rode after the pair –

to challenge the girl's father. Moshi struck out with his riding whip across Semah's face, nearly blinding him. When he realized the harm he had done, his heart softened. The lad was handsome, had embarked on a fine career and he was, in truth, an excellent match for Habibah. Moreover, Habibah herself expressed her willingness to marry Semah. And so, Moshi repented and gave his consent. The child went to live at the home of her fiancé's parents until she was 15, at which age a girl is considered ready for marriage in the Middle East. The union proved highly successful and produced eight children.

In her fifties, Habibah developed high blood pressure and became critically ill. The racial laws were becoming increasingly more severe. Four hundred of their fellow Jews had been killed in Baghdad in one single night. If the family remained in Iraq they too were threatened with extinction. Semah was often away on business and it was left to Habibah to organize the escape of the boys. Unfortunately, her physical condition had deteriorated, and one evening the doctor called Semah aside and told him it was unlikely that she would survive that night.

Semah walked out onto the roof-terrace and gazed up at the clear sky. My wife (then only 15) was in her bed on the terrace. Semah could not have noticed her for he addressed himself quietly to his God. She heard him say, 'I am 75 and have lived my span. My children now have greater need of their mother than of me. Please take from my years – and grant them to her.' My wife heard this and was forced to stifle her sobs.

Habibah *did* survive and put into operation the plan of escape for her children. When all but one of them had left the country, one evening Semah failed to return from his pharmacy. A sudden heart attack had taken him to his maker. Coincidence? Or the fulfilment of a pact? Only God knows.

❧

The Master of the Game

MY WIFE HAD SIX brothers, all of whom studied medicine. Their father, a pharmacist in Baghdad, had paid for their tuition in different cities and two of her brothers arrived in London to take the entrance exam at University College Hospital when, quite suddenly, their father died of a heart attack.

The brothers were called in separately by the examining board, to be told that, although both had passed the examination with flying colours, under the British quota system, only one person of their nationality could be accepted at the college. Albert's reply was that, as his brother was the older of the two, it was only fair that the place should be given to him. When Maurice was posed the same problem, his reply was, 'Take my younger brother. I'd like him to have the chance.'

The governing board were touched by the unselfishness of the two and they found a way to 'bend' the rules so that both could be accepted. But, with their father dead, how on earth were they to support themselves and pay their fees? A friend suggested they contact the Jewish Board of Guardians. There, it was discovered that a little-known fund had been established some years before by a Baghdadi benefactor, to enable young Iraqi Jews to study medicine in Britain. Moreover, the fund was to be channelled specifically to those studying at – guess where – University College Hospital!

Whoever moved their chessmen across the board of fate must have been a master of the game.

&

Roni

'HE'D HAVE BEEN better off dead.' How often have we said that of a child born with a severe handicap? But don't we really mean it would have been more convenient for *us* if he hadn't existed?

My wife's nephew Roni was born deaf. In most enlightened countries where organizations exist to help such people to learn to speak and to become self-reliant, this is a bad enough drawback as it is, but, in Iraq where Roni was born, such a misfortune is looked upon as a curse of God, and the fatalistic attitude of the people discourages them from doing much about it.

The reason for Roni's disability was simple and not uncommon. His mother had caught German measles while she was pregnant. But she never rationalized or accepted this: instead, she blamed God and her husband Elias. Most mothers develop a fierce, possessive love for their disabled infants and even lavish more attention on them than their other children. But not so Rebecca, Roni's mother. She tormented herself and her husband with remorse, until their life together became intolerable, and they separated. He took care of both boys, Roni and Dror, while she made her own way in life, free of any family encumbrances.

Elias earned an excellent living as an eye specialist and became head of the Eye Hospital in Baghdad. He saved the sight of a young member of the royal family and, as a result, he became almost the most honoured and respected man in the land. Everything money could buy was his for the mere effort of putting his hand to his pocket. His children had the most expensive education and lacked nothing their whim or fancy desired. By the age of 11, Roni could lip-read and make himself understood in Arabic, English and French. He shared his father's passion for motorcars, so Elias spent his free weekends taking the boys on long drives between the main cities of Iraq.

On one of these occasions, they were travelling at about 60 mph when Roni made frantic signs to his father to stop. When the car had slowed down almost to a halt, the rear end suddenly cranked down on one side and the car skidded over to land in a ditch. A wheel had come off. Elias asked Roni why he had so energetically signalled him to stop, and the boy explained in his flat, broken monotone that he could tell from the vibrations he felt in his cheek-bones that something unusual had occurred to a wheel of the car. Although deaf, he had succeeded in 'hearing' what normal ears had not detected – and in this way he perhaps saved the lives of his father and brother.

In ancient times, the Greeks killed children with deformities or known defects. Had we followed their lead, the world would have been poorer by the loss of Helen Keller, the deaf mute who learned to read and write, and lectured, wrote books and taught other children, and campaigned everywhere for a better understanding and treatment of such beings. She transformed our whole attitude towards this severe handicap.

Yes, in ancient Greece, the Helen Kellers and the Ronis would have been smothered at birth or their heads smashed against a wall. These days there are many who advocate the 'mercy killing' of the elderly and the decrepit, a step in the same direction. But perhaps God knows what He's up to, after all, and it is unwise to tamper with His elusive ways.

CB

A Yid

DURING THE WAR I was a staff sergeant in the British Army, in charge of a group of professional actors in uniform, performing for the British troops in Europe. When my mother heard that I was due to go to Germany, she filled a suitcase with tinned meats and various foods, hoping that I might have an opportunity of visiting one of the concentration camps which had only recently been liberated by the Americans and the British. As it happened, the camps had been sealed off by the Allies and none of us was yet permitted to enter. After two months of traversing much of the country, I was disappointed not to have come across a single Jew.

One afternoon, in Einbeck, I happened to be walking on a street pavement with my corporal when, out of the corner of my eyes, I vaguely noticed a middle-aged couple on the opposite pavement, walking in our direction. As we drew closer, for no reason I can think of, I found myself hesitating in the middle of a sentence and staring at the couple who were staring back at me. I was still talking to the corporal while I realized my feet were crossing the road towards the man and woman who simultaneously walked towards me.

The man shyly asked, 'A Yid? A Yid?' And there, in the middle of a busy main road, with cars hooting and swerving to avoid us, we embraced like long lost brothers, the tears streaming down our cheeks. They both bared their arms to show me numbers branded on their skin by the Aryan 'master race' which had enslaved much of Europe and given the world a new slant on genocide.

In British uniform, with an army beret on my head, I displayed no obvious characteristics or features of a Jew, so what could have made total strangers reach out to each other as we did? Was there not a hint of that brotherhood of man which our prophets and mystics of old instilled in our hearts? A momentary glimpse of the very mystery of being? Who knows? I know only that in a German city, on that December day, three people were drawn to cross a busy street towards each other by a mysterious magnet which made them weep, not with pain or sorrow, but with the happiness of recognition that there, in the wilderness of an Aryan land, among a nation which decimated my people, three Jews instinctively sensed each other out and joined hands in love and understanding.

CB

After Forty Years

*All right, so God doesn't exist and it's all done with mirrors!
And yet …*

HUNSDORF IS A small town in Hungary with a community of only a few thousand families in which there are no fewer than 20 people between the ages of 80 and 90. One of these, Abraham Yathom, has for 40 years been blind of both eyes, and his wife, who is over 100, has served as his guide for these many years.

As they grew older, Abraham's main worry was the fear that – by the laws of nature – she must surely be due to join her Maker before he. 'My love,' he would say to her, 'you have been my sight for nearly half a century. What will happen to me should God call you first? We have no children. Who will help me to dress, take me for walks and assist me in all things I cannot do on my own? What will I do without you?'

His wife never tired of reassuring him, 'Abraham, if I have

helped you, it is only because God willed it so. For 40 years, through me, He has not failed you. When I die, He will provide. Please have trust in Him.'

The day finally came when she failed to waken and Abraham knew that their lifelong companionship had ended. Panic seized him and for the rest of that day and night he remained in a state of shock, unable to turn his mind to the realization of what her absence would now mean to him.

Sleep is a blessed gift to troubled minds, and he finally succumbed. When he awoke some 14 hours later, the long, long night had departed not merely around him, but also from his eyes. The power of vision was restored to Abraham in its full vigour, and he could again see the rays of the sun flooding through the windows. This, after 40 years of blindness.

 endash

Izhak and Aziza

TO AN IRAQI, the most important event of his life is the birth of his first-born son. The continuance of his family line is reflected in the fact that people usually choose Biblical names and a man named Jesse would not be called that, but Abu Dahud – Father of David – even before he was married. David would be called Abu Sulman – Father of Solomon – and so on.

Aziza was 40 and had no children. Her husband Izhak had sent her to specialists and all had come to the same conclusion: no hope of ever giving birth. Aziza was resigned to this fact, but not so Izhak. To him, life was meaningless without a son to bear the family name and inherit the land which had been theirs for generations. Adoption was not the answer. It had to be a child of his own flesh and blood. The couple lived in Baghdad. Had they been Moslem, the answer would have been simple. Izhak could merely have taken a second wife to share the marital home and Aziza could raise no objections. However, they were Christian, and to them bigamy was repellent as well as forbidden.

Izhak was already 53 and consumed by his worry. Aziza feared for his health, and she made the most unselfish sacrifice a woman can. She insisted on his divorcing her and taking a younger, fertile wife. She was prepared to return to her parents' house and remain his shadow, while he satisfied his life's ambition to become a father.

At first, Izhak opposed the idea, but finally he gave in. A suitable bride of good family and upbringing was chosen by Aziza herself, and she left home. A baby was due within the year – a year in which Aziza had refused to see Izhak for his own sake, and the sake of the young bride. During the whole of the pregnancy Izhak's joy was mingled with regret. Aziza's absence was like an unhealing wound. He was kind and courteous to Jamila, his second wife, but there was no bond of love between them.

The day of the child's birth came and the midwife was sent for. As is customary in Iraq, the house was filled with relatives and friends awaiting the signal to rejoice. But when it came, it was a bitter moment. Jamila was delivered of a healthy boy, but she herself died. God gives, and God takes away.

As soon as she heard the news, Aziza had the child brought to her house to nurse him. After the traditional period of mourning, Izhak called at the home of Aziza's parents and took her and his son on a journey, back to his home. Across the threshold, he asked: 'Aziza ... will you be my wife?'

The child was not a child of her flesh, but he was the child of her love for Izhak: a love which alone knew how to rejoin the broken threads of their lives. Yes, God does take away, but He also gives.

Mummy

IN ISRAEL, I MET a woman who told me a rather moving story. She was one of a number of orphaned children in Austria whose parents were entirely wiped out by the Nazis and the little ones were secreted in a nunnery for safety. Later, the nuns were concerned as to what to do with them and a kind Catholic priest undertook to care for them. He baptized the children and began to teach them the tenets of Christianity. He was convinced that they had begun to lose the memory of their Jewish upbringing. After the war, a member of the Jewish Agency discovered the whereabouts of those orphans and came to claim them with the intention of transporting them to Israel. The priest refused to let them go, maintaining that the children were happy in their new belief and it would be cruel to confuse them with buried memories of extinct customs and traditions.

The representative of the Jewish agency argued that, however distant or buried in the subconscious minds of those little ones, the seed of their parents' creed was still alive and would regenerate. Finally, the priest offered a suggestion, 'I will grant you five minutes to convince the children. If you succeed, you may take them to Israel. If not, you must accept to leave them in peace with me.'

The woman agreed and went into the dormitory where the children were resting. She gently called out, 'Shema Yisrael, Adonai Elohenu, Adonai Ehad' ('Hear O Israel, the Lord thy God – the Lord is One', the first prayer a child learns at his mother's knee and the one recited on waking and going to sleep and at the moment of departing this earthly existence).

One after another the little ones began to cry out a single word, 'Mummy'. After that the priest graciously admitted defeat and the orphans were permitted to leave with the woman.

Part IV

Of People and Things

*'True stories are meant to be passed on.
To keep them to oneself is to betray them.'*

Elie Wiesel

Save My Son

M R PINCAS OF Wembley told me this amazing story. During the 1914–18 war, his brother was with the British Army, retreating from Marne in France. Their mother had a nightmare in which she dreamed of her son being up to his neck in mud. She screamed, 'Help my boy!' and awoke in panic.

It later transpired that, at that moment, the boy was crossing a bog and he slipped and fell up to his chin in mud. An Australian gunner – the last man in the platoon – heard a woman's cry and, turning, saw the lad about to drown in the mud. He held out his rifle to him and hauled him to safety. The platoon was captured by the Germans.

The lad was officially described as 'missing presumed dead', but the mother refused to accept this and continued to maintain that he was alive and would come back. That same gunner turned up at her home one day. He had been released in an exchange of prisoners, and he brought news of her son. The boy was alive and in the prison camp in Germany. Pincas's brother returned in 1919, fit and well.

CB

Cast Thy Bread …

'CAST THY BREAD upon the waters …' Cynics scoff at such Biblical advice. And yet … ?

Daniel Yusuf-Zade has an interesting story to tell. His grandfather, after whom he had been named, was born and bred in Bokhara. When still a lad, his father died suddenly, and among his papers the widow found a note to the effect that her husband owed a small sum of money to a man belonging to a Turkeman tribe near Meshed. 'The Torah tells us we should not rest our heads at night until all our debts have been paid,' said the widow of Yusuf-Zade, and she sent her young son on the long, arduous journey to search for the man and to repay the money.

Arriving at the village Daniel enquired after the Turkeman, only to be told he had died two weeks before. Daniel was directed to the home of the family and he offered the money to the widow.

'My husband never mentioned this debt. Besides he is gone now, so you owe us nothing.'

'No,' said Daniel. 'This is a debt of honour and must be paid. Please accept the money.' Daniel returned home and thought no more about the matter.

Many years later, now a married man with his own family, Daniel's village was attacked by a horde of bandits: one of those groups of marauders who prey on travellers crossing the borders of Afghanistan and who descend unexpectedly on isolated communities to rape, pillage and destroy. Daniel's home looked as though the locusts had invaded it. His family bunched into a corner of the room while he faced the thieves, silently watching them strip him of his possessions. It was useless to protest: that way led to certain death. At least, if he offered no resistance, there was a chance his family might survive the day.

The leader of the bandits had been staring at Daniel for a while and now approached him. 'Is your name Yusuf-Zade?'

'Yes,' he replied.

'A Jew.'

He swallowed hard. 'He knows my name and that I'm a Jew,' he thought to himself. 'Now I'm for it!'

'You don't remember me, Yusuf-Zade?'

'Should I?'

'Twenty years ago, when I was a boy, you called at our home in Meshed and left money to repay a debt from your father to a man who'd just died.'

'Perhaps ...' said Daniel, non-committingly.

'Well, I am the son of that man.' The brigand turned to his men. 'Put everything back. Nothing is to be stolen from the Jew's house ... and no one is to lay a hand on this man, his woman or children. They are under my protection. Understood?'

Probably Daniel lived to tell this tale because of his mother's strict Jewish principles. I doff my hat to you, widow Yusuf-Zade.

This true story was told me by the grandson of that same Daniel Yusuf-Zade, whose daughter Devorah is married to my eldest son Jonathan.

CB

A Lost Book

RECENTLY, I ATTENDED A lecture organized by the '45 Group, a 'club' of adults who were all children of parents gassed or murdered by the Nazis. These children survived the holocaust and were brought to England by a charitable

English Jew and have since made good, married, created their own families and formed themselves into a sort of mutual-aid society in which they assist the less fortunate members, take care of the families of those who have died, and donate large sums to various charities. A remarkable group of men who never let themselves forget that, but for a quirk of fate, they would now be ashes in the grate of the camp furnaces – like their parents before them.

The lecturer was himself a survivor of the Warsaw Ghetto and had a remarkable story to tell. It appears the Jewish doctors of the Ghetto decided to turn their misfortune to good account, and used to meet regularly to compare notes on the physical and mental effects of starvation and deprivation on their patients and themselves. A record was kept and all observations analyzed and documented.

The book was buried and never found by the Germans. After the destruction of the Ghetto and the liberation of Poland, it was salvaged and fell into the hands of the Russians who have never published nor released its contents despite numerous official and unofficial approaches. The contents of the manuscript could be of definite assistance to medicine, being an account of data not previously documented in such detail.

We may never be privileged to study the material, but the remarkable fact remains that Jewish doctors, in the midst of deprivation and extermination, should have been so unselfish as to take advantage of their plight, and offer to science the results of their firsthand experience. Just another proof of man's faith in tomorrow and the will to survive spiritually and mentally, even though the body was being destroyed.

CB

The Little Red Fawn

YOU KNOW THE sort of remark, 'The more I see of men, the more I like my dog!' You often hear people say they prefer animals to human beings. This, of course, is almost a blasphemous remark, but at times who among us has not felt in sympathy with it?

The actress Fay Compton once told me that she owed one of the most important stepping-stones of her career to an animal. It happened back in the 'twenties' when she was in Hollywood. She had been engaged to play an important part in an American film for a director who was reputed to be a tyrant. They were informally introduced and the director wasted no time in telling her what a fine performance *he* would make her give in *his* film under *his* direction. He was boastful, uncivil and domineering. And yet, there was a hint of kindness in his eyes. Fay described him to me as an overgrown child, play-acting at being important, but, at heart, complex and shy: capable of fooling everyone but himself.

They started work and it was soon evident he was a hard taskmaster, driving his technicians and artists to the point of distraction. Yet, he was artistically so meticulous, so painstaking in his search for perfection, that the atmosphere was vibrant with a kind of enthusiasm which forced people to give of their best, even though they risked a nervous breakdown in the process.

For some reason, he chose Fay as his chief whipping-boy, and he made her life so miserable that by the end of the first week, she was prepared to throw in the sponge. She sought an interview with the head of the company and asked to be released from her contract. He insisted she reconsider her request and arranged for her to have two free days in which to relax.

Her favourite recreation then was horse-riding. Fay

bundled her beautiful red setter Susan into the car, and set off early in the morning for the long drive out to the ranch at Pebble Beach, near Carmel. Hank, the stableman, knew her well and had already saddled the best runner, named Disraeli.

At Pebble Beach there is a magnificent ride known as the 'Thirty mile drive'. Fay mounted Disraeli and set off at a gentle trot together with Susan who loved to race ahead like a born hunting dog. They reached Bird Rock, an exciting spot where, on a calm day, you can see almost every seabird imaginable; then they rode on past the dense woods which reach the verge of the road.

Suddenly, without warning, a little red fawn leapt from the bushes and halted before them, quivering with the surprise of arrested motion. Disraeli pulled up sharply, and almost threw Fay over his head. Susan barked furiously at the fawn who remained completely unperturbed. Then, with a pretty toss of his little head, he advanced towards them, moving with ease and grace. Susan crouched on the ground and her bark changed to a menacing growl. Fay dismounted, calling to her to lie still. The fawn, wagging his tiny tail with eagerness, trustingly placed his nose close to the bitch's, sniffing in friendly greeting. Susan curled her upper lip in a threatening snarl, then slowly her body relaxed as she too sniffed enquiringly at the little stranger.

The fawn tossed his head again and playfully leapt backwards. Susan gave chase in and out of the bushes, and finally both came to rest close to Fay, who felt in her pockets for the sugar she normally kept for the horse, and offered one lump to each. The fawn took it from her hand so gently that Fay was moved to kneel and embrace the enchanting creature. He accepted her attentions, snuggling against her and nudging her pocket for another lump.

She kissed him goodbye, then mounted Disraeli and set off again, followed immediately by Susan. To her surprise the fawn joined them, trotting gaily by their side as though it were his daily routine. He followed them throughout the entire ride, head held high, leaping like a spring lamb thrilled to be alive. Fay too felt remarkably happy. Gone was the worry about the film and the difficult director, her concern about breaking her contract; she thought only of the surprising delight this sweet little animal had given her – merely by his presence.

On the way back, they reached the very spot where they first met him; the fawn halted abruptly and without another glance at them, leapt back into the woods as swiftly and suddenly as he had emerged. Fay returned to the ranch at Pebble Beach, a little saddened by her loss.

She mentioned the fawn to Hank as he helped her to dismount, and he smiled knowingly. 'Ah, Miss Compton,' he said, 'that means you must have a problem on your mind. That red fawn only ever seems to come to people who are in trouble. Seems to smell it out somehow. Very odd, no one's ever been able to account for it. "The Wise One" we call him.'

During the drive home, Hank's words lingered in Fay's mind. The recollection of the fawn's fearlessness in the face of danger, the disarming affection spontaneously offered to a snarling animal twice his size, crouched ready to spring, stirred her strangely. Was this perhaps the simple meaning of that greatest of all commandments, 'Love thy neighbour'?

She resumed work on the film with a new understanding. She boldly confronted the director, telling him she admired his talent so much that she forgave him his rudeness and ridicule; she hoped her performance would prove worthy of his direction; and she embraced him affectionately in the presence of the entire studio. From the tiny fawn, Fay had learnt to return warmth for distrust, friendship for enmity – and she found it worked wonders. From that moment, the two of them were the best of friends, and she did not hear another unkind word for the rest of the film – a film which, but for her encounter with the little red fawn, she would most certainly have abandoned.

Pet animals seem to know instinctively when their masters are sad or troubled, but how does one account for an incident such as this? On the face of it, Hank's explanation seems a little far-fetched. And yet? Isn't fact often stranger than fiction?

ᘓ

Anuccia

I F YOU ARE A father, you'll know the thrill you experience the very first time your baby says 'daddy'. But would you feel equally excited if it were to call you 'mummy' instead?

My Italian grandparents had 23 children of which my father was number 22. As though such a large family were not enough, they adopted a girl of four – the orphaned child of relatives who had died in a train crash. It's an odd story.

The child, Anuccia, had been sitting on her mother's lap when the train was hit by another and the carriage was ripped in two. Both parents died but Anuccia was protected by the body of her mother and survived without so much as a scratch. Whether because she missed her mother or because of the shock, for several weeks afterwards she remained morose, disinterested, unwilling to talk. She ate only when forced to and spent her waking hours staring at the floor or rocking herself backwards and forwards in slow motion. At the hospital, each nurse in turn tried to mother Anuccia: she took to none of them. Their attentions seemed only to annoy her.

My grandparents brought her to their home and lavished their love on her. The children offered their best toys and tried hard to make her join in their games. Anuccia just didn't care. Now and then her interest would be held by something, anc the others thought they had scored a hit. All too soon she wo uld return to her glum stare and to rocking herself to and fro. She was seen by doctors, specialists – all could offer no advice but patience. 'In her own good time she'll atune herself to her new surroundings, to the lack of her mummy and become the lively child she was before the accident. There is only one cure: love, love and more love,' they said.

For months, the situation hardly changed. Anuccia grew plump, but there was no 'go' in her, no fun, no joy. She was taken to the seaside, she was showered with a rocking horse, teddy bears, skittles, bricks, the score of conventional toys which appear in the shops with the regularity of the seasons. Any new one on the market was immediately bought by my grandfather and presented to Anuccia. All to no avail.

Even her own toys, fetched from her home, failed to please her. The only thing which brought any reaction was a shabby old blanket, found in her doll's cot. The wool had worn so thin that my grandmother almost threw it away. it was lucky she didn't. Anuccia clutched it almost savagely, and spoke her first word since the train accident. 'Ni,' she murmured, and put the corner of the blanket in her mouth. From then on, she showed it to everyone, telling them its name, 'Ni ... Ni ...'. She sucked it when she rocked herself and when she went to sleep at night. The family was thrilled. At last a breakthrough. They brought other articles from her home, hoping their familiarity might encourage her further. But their efforts were wasted: Anuccia had returned to her brooding. She would not be parted from the old blanket, day or night, and if ever it got mislaid, she became hysterical with panic.

My grandmother advised the family not to try so hard; to accept Anuccia's behaviour as a matter of course and leave her to come round in her own good time. But my grandfather refused to be beaten. It had become a challenge with him. Anuccia used to stare at him with what appeared to be dark resentment, and he was determined at all cost to break her resistance. He insisted Anuccia sleep in their bedroom, he almost neglected his own large brood, every free moment was spent with the child. He became tense, nervy and difficult to live with.

One day he was in the bathroom washing his hair when the door was pushed open and Anuccia appeared. My grandfather dried himself with the towel and wrapped it over his head, loosely holding the ends beneath his chin. As he turned, he noticed an unusual expression in her eyes For the very first time she appeared to be looking at h m with genuine recognition. She put out her right hand and touched the towel on his cheek. A hint of a smile came to her lips and she suddenly threw her arms round his neck and called out, 'Mamma!'.

Who knows what clicked in the child's mind at that moment? Perhaps the family likeness became more apparent when my grandfather's hair was covered, perhaps the act of washing his hair or putting a towel over it recalled to mind a familiar gesture of Anuccia's mother? Whatever it was, the ice was broken and in that instant Anuccia became a normal child again.

To be mistaken for a woman would hardly please any man – but, for my grandfather, it was the happiest moment of his life.

ജ

I am Innocent

'FAITH,' WE ARE TOLD, 'can move mountains.' My brother Ronald had an extraordinary experience in equatorial Africa during the war.

He had made friends with a native chieftain called Prince

Abula who had asked him to spend his leave from the Army Medical Corps at his village of Juda. While he was there, my brother was invited to attend the trial of two women accused of adultery. Although a man was allowed as many wives as his means permitted, the moral code in Juba was far stricter than in many more 'civilized' countries, and adultery was considered one of the most serious of all crimes. For this reason, Abula warned my brother not to expect any leniency in the justice he was about to witness.

The trial was held in the village clearing in the presence of the male population only. In the centre of the gathering was placed a cauldron of boiling oil. The two women were brought before the Elders and the prosecutor began to address them very quietly, like an orator anxious to command silence. Then his voice grew hysterical and he flung himself about in a comic frenzy. Apparently, the women were not permitted to speak in their own defence. Their innocence or guilt would be determined in a simple but hideously savage manner. Each in turn would have to thrust her right arm into the cauldron of boiling oil. If the arm was withdrawn intact and without pain, this would be proof of innocence. If, on the other hand, the flesh was burnt, this would be taken to be an admission of guilt, and the punishment for the crime would immediately be pronounced by the prosecutor.

Here, I would like to quote my brother's own words: 'At a sign from the prosecutor, the first woman slowly approached the cauldron and stood staring at it in horror. I felt desperate pity for her and glanced at Prince Abula, unable to believe that he would permit such a barbarous act to take place. His eyes seemed to warn me not to interfere, and for the moment I decided it was more prudent to acquiesce. The woman looked now as though she had steeled herself for the ordeal. She closed her eyes and raised her right arm. With one accord the jabbering tribesmen became silent. The woman started to tremble until her whole body was convulsed and I feared she would collapse. She lowered her arm to her side.

107

The crowd began to grow restless and several men cried out to her. She braced herself and raised her arm once again. Just as she seemed on the point of plunging it into the steaming liquid, she screamed aloud in abject terror and ran from the clearing straight into the surrounding jungle. The tribesmen broke into derisive jeers, but none attempted to catch her. I learnt later that it was part of the tribal code that anyone escaping or absconding from such a trial was never again permitted to enter the village, and, as often as not, was left to die in the jungle.

'The prosecutor then pointed to the second woman. Slowly, she walked forward to her accuser. She was by no means beautiful, but there was about her manner such pride and disdain that she compelled admiration. Unexpectedly she addressed the prosecutor. The Elders looked aghast at her presumptuousness and the prosecutor cut her short with a violent exclamation. The woman stood erect and seemed unafraid. She spoke quietly, without a hint of emotion, and I'd have given much to have been able to understand her language. She raised her arm above her head, and swiftly and suddenly thrust it into the boiling oil. A gasp arose from the throats of everyone present. She neither flinched nor uttered a murmur for a full three seconds I'd say. Then, slowly, she drew out her arm and held it high for the Elders to see. I give you my word, there was not a blemish or a burn. Not even the colour of the skin had changed. The Elders nodded their approval and she turned and displayed her arm to the crowd who screamed with delight.

'As long as I live I shall not forget the bravery of that woman. Trial by ordeal is of course not new to us. We in England used similar methods to try witches in medieval days. Could it be that in this primitive and seemingly inhuman trial lies a mysterious Truth, a source of spiritual values which our sophisticated civilization has crushed for us? I don't know. But I saw what I saw.'

A Good Investment

'DO YOU REMEMBER me? My name is Mr T—,' said the voice on the phone. 'I've been a radio fan of yours for years and you sent me a signed photograph. I met you once in the Charing Cross Road. You do remember me, don't you? The trouble is – I'm deeply embarrassed to tell you – but I've had terrible trouble getting somewhere for my young friend and me to sleep tonight. We've found a hostel in Willesden which can put us up, but they want five pounds and all I've got in the world is 20 pence. You do understand, don't you?'

I'd heard that kind of sob story often enough and my emotions had become almost immune by now, but this time the approach was unusual, and I must admit I found the accent attractive. 'Yes, I'll help you. If you're in Willesden now, catch a bus to my home – you've enough for the ticket with the 20 pence – and I'll give you the five pounds.'

Fifteen minutes later the front-door bell rang. Two men were there, both shabby and very wet from the rain. The older one introduced himself as Mr T—. 'I'm so very sorry to inconvenience you like this, but you do understand, don't you, sir? It's not for me you see, it's my young friend here. I can't let him sleep in the open yet another night. He caught himself a chill you see, and he can't … well, he can't exactly fend for himself, you do understand, don't you?'

I looked at the young man. He could have been anything between 17 and 26. Sallow complexion, eczema on his face, the hint of a first growth of soft stubble on his immature chin, and something odd in his manner: his eyes focused on nothing in particular, his head moved in a circular motion and a private smile hung on his lips.

I gave Mr T— an envelope containing the fiver he had requested plus enough for a day's food for them both and some fare money. I'm ashamed to say I was anxious to send them on their way before the barking dog brought my whole family to the scene.

'Mr Rietti, I'm expectin' an interview tomorrow for a job as a nightwatchman. If I get it, as true as I'm standing here, I'll pay you back. You see if I don't. But, if I don't get the job, I'll give you a word of advice worth far more. I know you're a Jew and it was your people who taught us to love our neighbour. But, believe me, it's not enough to love people. You've got to learn to love inanimate things. They need our love and attention just as much. You try it, sir. You'll see your affection will rebound off them, like an echo.'

He walked away, then turned back and added, very earnestly, 'You do understand – this lad is everything in the world to me, and I love him dearly. He's a little simple and we need each other. Like your dog there, he asks nothing of anybody. He's rich because he's content with what he has got. He doesn't fret over misfortune: he's just happy to be alive. Well, goodnight to you.'

They were gone. I could have given them a plate of hot soup or some food to take away, but I hadn't. I merely gave them money I could afford and sent them packing as fast as I could. I suddenly felt ashamed.

I took the car and drove to Willesden on the off chance of coming across them, but of course I did not. On the way back, I thought of the advice he'd given me, and I tried it out on the gear lever. This had given me a lot of trouble especially in cold weather, and I tended to anticipate resistance and treat it roughly. Now I tried a new tactic. I thought of its vital importance as it engaged the gears and set the wheels in motion, and I tried to show it affection. I eased it gently forward and back and, do you know something? It moved in and out of gear with great ease! Since then, I've tried it on stubborn locks, on doors which jam, on unyielding screws, on countless things. And it really works.

Who knows if Mr T— was genuine, or just a conman using his unfortunate companion to gain sympathy and cash?

It doesn't matter. He offered far more than he took and those few pounds I thrust into his hand were one of the best investments I've ever made!

CB

A Kind Lady

M Y RUSSIAN grandfather, Moshe Rosenay, owned a flourishing furniture store in Brestlitovsk and his clientele consisted in the main of the well-to-do army officers and their families. For a Jew to survive in business during the Czar's regime he had to know how to parry the barbed thrusts and harsh insults frequently aimed at him by his non-Jewish neighbours.

For example, on one occasion a drunken colonel had entered the store, brandishing his sword, and grabbed my grandfather by the throat, 'You dirty Jew ... your people killed our Saviour!' He forced my grandfather to his knees and drew back his sword to thrust it into him. Struggling for breath, my grandfather replied: 'I assure Your Excellency that, had I been there, I would not have allowed him to die!' The Russian officer was so amused, he sheathed his sword and embraced my grandfather like an old friend.

Moshe Rosenay was impulsive and often made important decisions without consulting his wife. On one occasion, he left home early, taking only his umbrella and hat, and said he'd be back to dinner. Two months later the family received a letter from New York, telling them he had gone to 'sound out the possibility of their emigrating there'.

On another occasion, he closed the business, sold up everything and announced the family were off to Palestine with the early wave of pioneers. At the station, aside from their relatives, numerous young women turned up to bid the family a safe journey. They were total strangers to him, but all embraced his wife and seemed genuinely distressed at her departure.

'Fania, who on earth are they?' he asked her.

'Oh, just some young friends,' she mumbled.

Not satisfied with her reply, he asked one of them how she came to know his wife.

'Mrs Rosenay introduced us to our husbands and gave us dowries to help us start up our home,' she told him.

It appears that, over the years, Fania had surreptitiously saved from her housekeeping money and the extra sewing she took in, in order to arrange the weddings of poor young women in Brestlitovsk. They say 'Charity begins at home', but she looked on every fellow Jew as her family. Can there be a better example to follow?

☙

The Ticket

'SHE FELL DOWN a few moments ago and no one gave her a hand,' said the cloakroom attendant. I had just helped to lift an elderly woman from the floor to a chair. It was at a theatre in the north-west of London on a Sunday night The place was packed with people who had paid well to support a visiting foreign company performing in aid of charity. The curtain was due to rise at any moment, and the latecomers were too busy to notice the less spectacular drama taking place by the cloakroom.

I picked up the woman's glasses and scarf and put them in her open handbag. She closed it herself and it was then I noticed that only her left hand was able to move. The other lay inert in her lap. 'Mm … a stroke,' I thought. She must have been in her early seventies, grey-haired, face lined; her large soft eyes staring vacantly from under lids which kept closing and opening slowly as though she were emerging from sleep. I questioned her. No response. I tried French, then Italian. Her only answer was to show me her theatre ticket. I placed my hand on her forehead and stroked her hair. Her lips broke into a smile – so sweet and trusting that in that moment she looked nearer 17 than 70.

The attendant phoned for an ambulance and returned with a young man. He recognized her. 'Oh yes, she came to the booking-office this afternoon and could only speak German. Someone else understood a little and said the woman was anxious to buy a ticket. We had only a few expensive ones left and she seemed thrilled she was in time to buy one.'

The ambulance arrived and we helped her into the canvas chair the two men brought for her. As they carried her expertly up the stairs, she did not take her eyes off me. Later, I checked with the hospital: she was comfortable but still unable to speak. Her handbag had revealed no name or address.

I went to visit her and tried to talk to her in my few words of German. Nothing registered. She stared vacantly and what emerged from her lips was mere sound without meaning. Three days later, her identity remained as mysterious as the night of her collapse. No one had made enquiries about her either at the theatre or through the police.

I visited her again and took with me a pot of red cyclamen. She was in a wheelchair, about to be taken for a walk. She sat immobile, lost, completely disinterested in her surroundings. I noticed her left hand was clenched. I placed the flowerpot on the table of her wheelchair. She accidentally knocked it over. I started to stand it upright again, but she pushed my hand away and straightened it herself, then felt the pot all around and touched the flowers rather as a blind person might, but with her fist still half clenched. She looked up at me and her eyes seemed for the moment less vacant. She attempted to speak, but again only gurgling sounds came from her lips. My heart went out to her. Imagine the torment that must go through such a mind, still partially active, still sending commands through the nerves to that part of her body as yet unable to react; a mind struggling to enunciate, to explain, to communicate, but wholly unable to. Was she destined to remain unidentified? Anonymous?

She screwed up her eyes and the muscles of her face went tense. I put one hand on her forehead and caressed her hair with the other. She began to relax, then slowly smiled: the same trusting, ingenuous smile she had given me when I made that particular gesture the night I found her at the theatre. Had she recollected it? Had something finally clicked in the darkened recesses of her mind?

Eagerly I said in German, 'Sonntag? Theater? Verstehen?' I think she did understand. She made a sign with her hand. I gave her paper and pencil. She took it between her thumb and forefinger and in uneven letters she began to write a man's name and address in Hamburg. The silence had been broken.

The name she wrote proved to be her son's. He flew over to be with her and assist in her recovery. But fate is cruel – or perhaps kind? That name and address were the last words she wrote. She died in her sleep two days after her son's arrival. Peacefully and silently. When they unclenched her fist they found in it the crumpled ticket for the Sunday-night show she had wanted so much to see.

Perhaps the excitement of its anticipation had brought on the stroke in the first place. Perhaps she died, still believing she was soon to see the dancers and singers and dared not part with the expensive ticket she had bought, and her mind had stopped at that moment of happiness. She was old and sooner or later death was inevitable. Perhaps, after all, she had picked a fine moment to buy her ticket for the final journey to her Maker.

It is Well

DURING THE GREAT Chicago fire of 1871, Horatio Spafford, a prosperous American lawyer, lost most of his property and, after the work of reconstruction had taken toll of his wife's health, he decided to give her a holiday in Europe. He had some business to conclude so he sent her and their four children on ahead in the passenger steamer *Ville du Havre*.

In mid-ocean, at two o'clock in the morning, a sailing vessel ran into the steamer and cut it in two. Within twelve minutes the *Ville du Havre* had sunk. There were only a few survivors, and when these finally reached Cardiff, Horatio Spafford received a telegram from his wife made up of only two words: 'saved – alone'.

Horatio immediately left Chicago and journeyed to comfort his wife and accompany her home. One day during the crossing, the captain pointed out that they were probably passing over the very place where Horatio's four children had drowned. He lent over the rail and lost himself in meditation. He was a religious man, not given easily to weeping. Instead, he composed a prayer:

> *It is well with my soul.*
> *When peace like a river attendeth my way,*
> *When sorrow like sea-billows roll,*
> *Whatever my lot, Thou hast taught me to say:*
> *It is well, it is well with my soul.*

Later, the Spaffords were blessed with a baby son and then another girl. Happiness again had meaning for Mrs Spafford. But, within a year, both children caught scarlet fever – and the little boy died.

This new misfortune would have been enough to destroy

many parents, but Horatio took this to be a sign from on high, and, after their seventh child Grace was born, he took his now small family to the Holy Land in search of peace of mind, and a way to serve other beings more unfortunate than themselves.

They rented a large house built above the Jaffa Gate, the highest point in Jerusalem, and before long the 'Little American Colony' was known for its Samaritan work among the poor and sick. During the 1914–18 war they turned the house into a hospital where they nursed both Turkish and British soldiers and, after the armistice, it became a school of handicrafts and dressmaking for girls. That might have been the end of the story but for something strange which occurred on Christmas Eve in 1925.

Bertha, Horatio's elder daughter, was leaving the house to lead the carol singing at Bethlehem when she met a woman, desperately ill and carrying a tiny baby, being helped up the road by her husband. As it was Christmas, the Government Hospital was closed to out-patients and he could get no help. Bertha was strangely touched as she considered that here she was, off to sing carols to commemorate the birth of the baby who was born in a stable because there was no room at the inn, and there, before her, stood another rustic madonna in almost the same plight. Bertha went to the hospital and made sure that the woman was comfortably settled and the baby bathed and fed.

Next morning, the father returned with the babe in his arms. His wife had died in the night. 'I live in a damp cave,' he explained. 'If I take my baby there, he will die. Please save my son.' How could Bertha refuse? Soon words spread that Allah had sent a ministering angel to tend to needy orphans, and, within a week, she was saddled with two more. From that it was only one step to becoming a regular, recognized children's hospital. And for over 40 years it served the Arabs of the Old City and the surrounding villages. A million-and-a-half patients were treated in the 'house on the wall'.

Teddy Kolleck, the Mayor of Jerusalem, arranged for the grounds outside the house to be granted to the Spaffords on condition that it was turned into a playground for the Arab children. Today, it is the *only* playground in the entire city where children can gather out of the bustle and danger of the streets. Perhaps from this union of Christian family, Israeli Mayor and Arab children springs the true message of the Bible 'Love thy neighbour'.

છૂ

Little Franc

A FEW YEARS AGO, I was working on a film in Yugoslavia and the company was staying at a hotel on Katarina Island, which is a short ferry-trip from Rovinj on the mainland. There are many such small islands dotted around the coast – not all of them inhabited – and when Nadia Gray, our leading lady, had a free day, she would hire a fisherman to row her out and go exploring. On her return, she would tell us of her 'finds' that day. She was most entertaining and not given to exaggeration.

She said she was searching for an island to buy for herself, and, at last, she announced she had found the ideal place – a wholly deserted island no larger than a small suburban park, about three-quarters of an hour's row from Katarina. It was promptly nicknamed 'Nadia's Island' and the company was jestingly forbidden to set foot on it.

Knowing my zest for quiet places in which to write, Nadia one day offered to share her 'treasure find' with me and I was rowed out to it. It was indeed an enchanting isle, thickly overgrown with vegetation, with hidden little beaches, nooks and crannies, and the ruins of a monastery.

117

I have always been attracted to ruins. I like to sit on the remains of a stone wall, or marble column hundreds of years old and picture to myself the surroundings, its people, their hopes, longings, manners and behaviour. I often have the comforting sensation that I am far from being alone, even though the silence and peace around me remain undisturbed.

The monastery was situated in a clearing, surrounded on all sides by bushes and trees. To reach it, we'd had to wade through thick undergrowth which clearly had not been disturbed at all that summer. But, on the far side of the building, one could see a narrow path leading into the bushes. Nadia decided to sunbathe on the grass while curiosity guided me along the path. It led steeply down then, just as steeply, it climbed again, the growth abruptly giving way to a clearing. I found myself at the cliff-edge, overlooking rocks and the open sea. On a ledge just below me was a stone cross, the only sign of one-time habitation on the island other than the monastery. I climbed down to examine the cross and found it bore no words, merely a date: 1878. The peacefulness surrounding it was impressive and I could easily understand why a man would wish to be buried there.

On the way back, I began to muse on the absence of words on the cross, and I decided it must be the grave of a monk who wished to die anonymously as he might have lived in his contemplative seclusion. But then, I started to wonder about the well-cared-for path which led directly from the monastery to his grave. This could not have been coincidence. If the man had died over a hundred years ago, the person responsible for this show of tidiness could certainly not have been a contemporary of his, for over three generations had passed since the event. At most, it could be a grand, or great-grand nephew. Rather unusual, I thought, for anyone to go to such lengths of devotion after so many years.

Back on Katarina Island, I made enquiries, but no one could help me. Everyone knew these small islands but few bothered to visit them or learn their history. I was told to look for the fisherman called Dondo Lujo on the mainland. He was the local 'know-all' who, if anyone, might be able to enlighten me.

I found Dondo Lujo. He smiled at my questions and told me an extraordinary story, which had been handed down from father to son, to son. Among the community of monks who once inhabited the island, had been one whose love of birds had earned him the nickname 'The Little Franc' (after Saint Francis of Assisi). He had been responsible for the gardens of the monastery which were known for their variety of plants and bushes brought from different countries. It was he who made the path which led to the cliff-edge on the north side of the building. To tend it, Little Franc did an amazing thing: he enlisted the help of the birds. He taught them to pick out weeds and to carry away the leaves which gathered. This habit – once acquired – had been passed on by the parent birds to their young, and continued uninterrupted to this day.

'Little Franc' may no longer be remembered by man, but his love for the fellow creatures who share God's earth will reap a rich reward as long as the birds remember his teaching and continue to impart it to successive generations. Could he have a more fitting epitaph?

❧

She Lights Two Candles

'I HOPE YOU DON'T mind my having brought my little boy with me, but my wife is away and I had no one to leave him with today,' said the taxi-driver. I was in Paris, on my way back to London, and had rung for a taxi to take me to the airport. The driver turned out to be Portuguese, and my 'antennae', as ever, were at the ready to pick up an interesting story.

Jaime told me that when he was eight years of age (the eighth son of parents living in a village near the Spanish border), his father could not get work locally, so he found a job in Spain. On Fridays, with his wages, he would buy a sack of coffee, carry it on foot 12 miles to home, sell the coffee, and, with the proceeds, the family would eat well over the weekend and he'd leave his wife money for the rest of the week while he returned to work across the border.

The local priest denounced him to the police as being a bad Catholic because he never attended Mass. The man was arrested, thrown in jail, and 'mysteriously' found dead two days later. This left the widow with eight mouths to feed – and no breadwinner.

Tragedy seldom strikes singly. Their neighbour had coveted their little plot of land for some time, and now she seized her chance. She, too, went to the police, falsely claiming that Jaime's mother had set fire to her barn. The widow was taken to court, convicted, and sentenced to eight years' imprisonment.

And the children? Good neighbours settled them with friends and distant relatives, and Jaime was sent to Paris to be brought up by a French family.

Many years later, Portuguese friends of Jaime decided to visit their native land and persuaded him to go with them. At a seaside town, late one evening they entered a restaurant, intending to order a meal – but the place was about to close. However, the waitress told them she would prepare something herself. When they had eaten, out of gratitude, they invited her to join them for coffee. She listened to Jaime talking and remarked, 'You have an excellent pronunciation of Portuguese.' Jaime explained that he had been born in Portugal but left as a child and had forgotten much of his mother-tongue. When he mentioned the name of his village, the woman's eyes lit up.

'But I come from there! What's your name?'

He told her – and the waitress fainted. When she came to, Jaime discovered she was none other than his very own mother. He then told me he took her back to Paris to live with his family and devoted the next two years to search for his brothers and sisters, and he eventually traced all seven of them.

I asked Jaime what was his surname and he replied, 'Pereira'.

'I know several Portuguese Jews with that surname. Are you Jewish by any chance?'

Jaime looked shocked. 'Good Lord, no. We are all staunch Catholics.'

But I was not prepared to let it go at that. 'Are there any odd customs your mother keeps which she perhaps does not even understand?'

He thought for a moment. 'No. Oh yes – there is one! Every Friday evening my mother lights two candles in a little box. She doesn't know why – but she does it because her mother did and her mother before that ... so it became a sort of tradition in the family.'

I smiled to myself as I explained that during the Holy Inquisition in Spain and Portugal Jews often had to hide the fact that they were of the hated religion and on Friday nights the woman of the house would light the two Sabbath candles secretly in a little box so that they could not be seen from the street.

I paid him his fare and offered his little boy a ten franc piece.

'Please don't do that Monsieur', the man stopped me. 'I have taught him not to accept gifts from strangers.'

'Signor Pereira, I think you'll find we are not exactly strangers.' I told him, 'I believe we both have the same ancestors in Abraham and Moses.'

I left Monsieur Pereira looking as pale as a sheet!

Frank

Don't ever let us part
For that will break my heart
And a broken heart is useless as you know
For we promis'd from the start
That we would never part
And that promise I will keep, I love you so

You're my life, my joy and flower
You were sent from in power
To surround me with a love so warm and true
And with my eyes closed I can hear
Your sweet voice of love my dear
Yes, my darling, O my darling I love you.

THAT POEM WAS written by an ex-convict called Frank who strove against impossible odds to keep his family together. Frank had been to jail ten times and his wife and six children found themselves at the dead end of the road. No roof over them, in debt to the roots of their hair, poverty so dense that, once again, stealing seemed the simplest way out.

Oh, yes, Frank knew the deep despair we force on the rejects of our society: but while in prison he began to express himself in poetry, and, beneath his unhappiness, he found the seed of something enriching. He put into words two emotions: the very real love he felt for his wife, and praise. Praise for some Presence in the universe he sensed was there for the reaching.

Here is one of the poems in which he tried, in his simple way, to describe that Presence he called, 'the Friend':

Some people laugh
For they don't care
They think it's mad
To say a prayer

Which don't take long
When you want to know
The right from wrong.
So say your prayer
And speak your mind
The Friend will help you
This you will find.

You can take my freedom
You can take my wealth
But that won't mean the end
You can tie me down
You can shut me up
But you can't take away my Friend.

And when I leave this world behind
I will go and join my Friend.
He is the only Lord in the world
The only Lord I believe in
And nothing in this world of yours
Will change my mind.

After going straight for nearly three years, Frank died in a tragic road accident, leaving those six children with no great legacy except the Friend who understood his problems better than anyone he knew.

ॐ

Manasseh

I F EVER YOU find yourselves in Avignon, that medieval French city of the Italian popes, take a car-ride 15 km out to the little town of Carpentras.

'Why Carpentras,' you may ask, 'it's barely mentioned in the guide books? What is there that's special about it, except perhaps the Roman arch which has no unusual feature to recommend it?' No, it's not the arch which should draw you to Carpentras. It is another link with the past – a small synagogue, built 600 years ago. Once it was the centre of a busy community of shopkeepers, tailors, craftsmen and tradesmen. Today, only 21 Jewish families remain.

Last summer, I paid a visit to Carpentras and called at the synagogue. I sentimentalized over the once-white walls, the worn wooden benches, wrought-iron candelabra, the Minister's platform above my head, the women's gallery behind the criss-cross screen, the enchanting little circumcision chair hanging on the wall, the 25 Scrolls of the Law (one-and-a-quarter to each family), and something within me grew sad. Here was my past: here my people had gathered every Friday eve to welcome the Sabbath bride: here countless cantors had led their congregations in prayers of thanksgiving and praise; those wooden benches obtained their shine from innumerable coats, inadvertently polishing the seats as their owners rose and sat as the liturgy demands.

I followed the stone steps down to the well deep in the bowels below, and found myself next to the Mikveh, the ritual bath. The beadle was acting as guide to a small group of Frenchmen, Spaniards and Americans. 'Here come the women for their monthly purification, and here the good earth thrusts forth its liquid freshness in a limpid pure stream, look, my friends – it is so clear that you can see your faces reflected below. Hold that child, please, the steps are dangerous, and the water is deep!'

'Did the Germans close the synagogue during the war? Did they take away the Jews?' an American asked.

The guide was reluctant to say. 'I ... I was not here. Come now with me to see the synagogue. Ah, we have a new visitor. Won't you join us?'

'Thank you, I have already seen it,' I told him.

'Then if you'd like to wait here, I'll return shortly and show you the bakery.'

'Thanks. I'll wait.' Their footsteps echoed slowly away and I sat alone in the cool, stone cellar. Alone with the ghosts of my past.

Recalling Dr Brunler's theory, I am convinced that each of us bears his own aura, a form of radiation which affects everyone with whom we come in contact, and that every single thing we touch bears the imprint of our personalities for as long as there are people sensitive enough to receive these vibrations. I believe that we can conjure up a feeling and an atmosphere which has clung to the rooms, the walls, the furniture of the people who once loved, touched, breathed, laughed and suffered in those rooms. Because of this, when visiting a new place, I often sit in silence, with eyes closed, my fingertips touching the furniture which once supported other beings, heard other tongues, shared other secrets. I let my mind relax, hoping to sense – if not receive – some of the radiations those personalities of the past have left around me.

On this occasion I sat on a stone bench, and my fingers wandered into the crevice between the back of the seat and the wall. It encountered something smooth and hard. It was a small stone, almost perfectly round, which rested in my palm like a tiny creature, nestling for human comfort. I closed my eyes and let my senses drift in search of the radiations. Did I sleep? I don't know, but in the corner of the cellar, I could dimly make out a shape emerging from the shadows. A long cotton coat hanging loosely on bowed shoulders. Pale, hollow cheeks and wispy beard beneath a black round-rimmed hat. And from the sunken sockets there shone a pair of transluscent eyes – gentle, dreamy, totally in contrast with the man's general appearance. He stared at me for as long as I dared hold his gaze, then beckoned me to follow him as he turned, and merged into the wall!

Was I dreaming? I hadn't moved, yet my body seemed to

leave me behind as it started forward in response to his gesture. Once through the wall, I found myself in a classroom where some 30 boys were at their wooden desks. All wore hats and the sideburns of ultra-orthodox students. Before them stood the same man I had just seen in the cellar. I looked around me at the boys – earnest, eager, tired faces, starved of fresh air and sunlight. As I stared, they seemed to change before my eyes. To change into adults, emaciated men whose bones pierced their unhealthy-looking skin. Evil-looking numbers had been branded into their flesh. The numbers of Auschwitz, Buchenwald, Treblinka. I looked back at their teacher. He was speaking to them gently but with great authority. I took my place among those living skeletons, and listened as attentively as they.

He spoke without bitterness of their suffering, conjuring up memories of a better life before those numbers were burned into their arms. From their expression I could see they were reliving the recollection of their homes, their families, their loved ones. Then he turned to the future. 'You all dream of the Messiah. You picture Him above in the heavens. But He is actually here, on this earth with you. You believe He is untouched by the agonies which beset you, that He is sheltered from harm, but in reality He shares your suffering, the sadness that surrounds you, the pain of the cudgels which smash into your faces. The deprivation you are made to undergo engulfs Him, too. He encourages you not to despair. Let me tell you He has greater need of you than you of Him. Do not abandon Him. You must ensure that He is not the only one of His people to survive.' That word reverberated round the entire room. 'Survive ... survive ... survive!'

The speaker paused and looked deeply at each and every one present. They had remained still and silent, mesmerized by that man who seemed to know the secret of why we came into this world and why we depart.

I opened my mouth to speak, I wanted to urge him not to

stop, to continue inspiring us, to 'take us back where everything began, where the world lost its innocence and God lost His mask', but no words came to my lips. It was as if he understood my need, for he addressed himself directly to me.

'God is eternal only because we make Him so. As the Good Book tells us, "By accepting suffering and death, man creates the eternity of his creator".

'When they take your father, your wife, your son – your despair is His. "Why?" you will ask of Him. "Where is the logic in that?" What matters then, my son, is not that two and two make four – that is logical – but that God is One. Only then will you realize what I have learned: that survival is not only essential – it is possible!'

The others turned to stare at me. Their death-like eyes pierced the very core of my being, and fear suddenly drenched me in sweat. I cried out, 'Don't stare at me, I don't belong here, I'm not one of you, you all died in the gas chambers. I'm alive. I'm not ashes … not dead … not dead … not dead! I'm not here … not here … not here. Alive … alive … alive!'

My words choked me and I could no longer breathe. I clenched my fists and beat my forehead to drag myself from the nightmare. It was then that my brain seemed to burst out of me and past and present were confused so that I was no longer conscious of where I was nor in which time I existed. Only his face remained clear before me, gazing with deep compassion into my innermost self.

'Who are you? Who are you?' I asked as he began slowly to recede from my consciousness.

'My name is not important, but they call me Manasseh.'

I was aware of someone shaking my shoulder and I opened my eyes. The synagogue guide was standing before me. 'I'm sorry I was so long. They asked many questions. Do you want to see the bakery?' I followed him like an automaton, not listening to his monotonous patter – my mind was with another. I interrupted his flow.

'Who is Manasseh?'

The guide stopped talking and looked at me intensely. 'You could not have known him. You are too young.'

'Who was he?' I insisted.

The guide was sad now and his eyes focused on distance. 'Manasseh was our Hebrew teacher, a Talmudic scholar. During the war, when the Germans came for us, it was he who hid the Sifrei Torah, the Scrolls of the Law, to preserve them. And when we were carted off in cattle-trucks to the concentration camps, he took with him only his prayer shawl and phylacteries, and a handful of round stones, which he always collected – it was an odd habit of his. When they took Manasseh to the gas chamber, he gave me his stones and he said, "If you survive, remember that life is as round as these stones. You end where you begin. And you recommence where you have ended."

'You ask who was Manasseh? He was a saint. He kept alive our hope and our belief in man. I could have lived happily in Israel after the war, but I came back to the synagogue because I could not desert his memory.' He added, almost inaudibly, 'And out of a sense of guilt because I was spared and he was not.'

The guide seemed suddenly to be ashamed of having said too much. 'But why do you ask?' he said. 'How did you know about Manasseh? There's no one left here but myself to remember him.'

I looked down at the stone which still lay in my hand and I closed my fingers over it to hide it from the other's view. 'I'm afraid I must go,' I said, and gave him some francs for his pains.

'Oh, merci … for the synagogue funds,' he murmured. 'Au revoir, Monsieur. Come again.'

Come again? I don't know that I dare. There are times when I tell myself it was all a dream, a figment of my imagination, until I pick up that stone and feel its smooth round surface in my hand. Shall I ever forget Manasseh? I don't think I can.

ॐ

Remembrance –
a Yom Kippur Meditation

YOM KIPPUR – the Day of Atonement. What will run through my mind as that eerie sound disturbs the fibres of my being at the end of the synagogue service? That ram's horn whose blast reverberates through the dark reaches of the universe? It is an alarm, as it was for the tribes of Israel in the desert when the enemy approached, and for the armies of David and Solomon. An alarm awakening the soul to judgement.

But before judgement comes repentance, and before that – remembrance. And who has cause to remember if not the Jew? Was not Israel called 'The Bride of God'? Was she not chosen out of grace, not for her greatness or goodness, but simply because God wanted it that way? 'You *only* have I chosen of all the families on earth: therefore I will punish you for all your iniquities.' Oh yes – there is a shadow cast by every brightness, a sadness that follows the joy. And the greater the privilege, the greater the responsibility.

What will my remembrance be on that holy day? First, the recollection that it was my people who gave mankind its greatest law, 'You shall not hate your brother in your heart, but you shall reason with your neighbour, lest you bear sin against him. You shall not take vengeance or bear grudge against the sons of your people, but you shall love your neighbour as yourself.' As yourself? Three thousand years after that commandment enriched mankind, in Munich, 11 men in the bloom of their youth were butchered.

I will remember that it was our prophets who taught that God did not ask for synagogue or church or mosque services, but that we should share our bread with the poor, that we should clothe the naked, do justice and love mercy. Love mercy? One Tuesday, in Munich, but a few years ago, in the darkness of a military airfield, after two had already died, nine of my people were butchered.

I will remember that the blessing of Sabbath, the day of rest, was gifted the world through us; that Hebrew Laws were specially designed to protect the widow and the fatherless, for they were particularly dear to God. That it was an Israelite who taught mankind that there must be one law for all men: the same for the Jew and the foreigner within his gates. Was ever racism more firmly banished from any society?

I will remember that it was a Jewish scientist, Abraham bar Hiya, who first translated Greek and Arabic works into Latin, and who developed the first scientific methodology. That another of my people, Emanuel Bon-Fils, invented the decimal system 150 years before it was accepted in Europe, that his astronomy tables guided the mariners of the fourteenth century. That yet another, Levi Ben Gerson, created the basis for modern trigonometry and invented the 'Jacob's staff' which aided Magellan, Columbus and Vasco da Gama. I will remember that the contributions of Rosenzweig and Buber shaped existentialism, that Freud and Einstein revolutionized the modern mind. I will remember that two-thirds of the civilized world are governed by the ideas of my people: the ideas of Moses, Hillel, Jesus, Paul, Spinoza, Marx.

And the remembrance of this will help me to hold my head erect, not with false pride, but, paradoxically, with the pride of the humble, as I join my fellow Jews in prayer and repentance. Dear God – '*thou* delightest not in the destruction of the world'. But what of men? I will remember that a few short years ago, 11 of my people who represented their nation in the peaceful sports of the world, in the bloom of their youth, were butchered.

ଔ

We Light these Candles ...

A N EMINENT publisher who had become totally assimilated and thought no more of his Jewish traditions than he did of yesterday's discarded garbage was driving to work in his expensive limousine, when he turned on his car radio to listen to the news. He happened by chance to hear one of my talks on the Sabbath which was being broadcast just before the important events of the day.

The reference to my mother lighting the Shabbat candles on Friday nights and the happiness on her face as she turned to the family and bade us 'Shabbat Shalom' stirred a distant memory in the recesses of his mind. He glanced at his watch, turned his car around and drove straight to the auction rooms where that very morning various unwanted articles, left to him by his parents and which had gathered dust over the years as they lay unused and uncared for, were being auctioned.

He arrived in time to retrieve his mother's silver candlesticks, brought from Russia when she and his father had emigrated from the land where they had lost all their relatives in one of the more severe pogroms under the Czar's regime. Those candlesticks had been passed from mother to daughter for generations and his own mother had gifted them to his bride some 30 years before.

The publisher's wife wrote to me to tell me of this incident. She said that since that day those candlesticks have occupied a place of honour at their Friday evening meal and, although they do not keep all the mitzvoth as they would wish, every Shabbat eve she undergoes the thrill of an emotional experience she finds it hard to define as she lights the candles placed in those very candlesticks, in honour of a tradition she had been the first to break after centuries of family observance.

This information gave me greater satisfaction than anything I can recall in many a year, and proves to me that if we can only tap the dormant memories which lie in the subconscious mind of every assimilated Jew, we can bring back to him the true joy of Judaism which is there for the mere asking.

CB

It's Forbidden to be Old

'IS THAT YOU, Robert? Ronald, here. Sad news, I'm afraid. Papa died last night.'

Those of you who have lost a father will know the impact those words from my brother on the telephone had upon me. The sudden catch in the throat, the loss of breath, the numbness of all feeling. No tears – just emptiness. So Papa is dead!

Forty years before, when he was a vigorous, active 35, his heart threatened suddenly to pack up. The doctor gave him six months to live. He outlived that doctor and crammed to the brim an eventful life. He had been actor, playwright, poet, theatre administrator, director, violinist, conductor and teacher. He had imparted knowledge to countless students and professionals in various forms of art. He was known to all as 'Papa Rietti'. Somehow he had seemed eternal. It was unthinkable that there could ever be a day without Papa. Yet that day had come, and he was no more. No more? Doesn't that imply the seizing up, the cutting off, the termination of existence, the end? Is that what I mean? At first it seemed so.

Papa's fortitude had been incredible. At 60 he fell in front of a bus which crushed his leg. Three months later the leg fractured again, and after a second operation he was enveloped in plaster from neck to feet. During the ten months he lay flat, he wrote a play and a book of poems in French. He returned home on crutches. When a phone call came for him to appear in a film, Mother refused to let him go. We heard a terrible clatter on the staircase and rushed there, fearing the worst. There was Papa, at the top of the stairs, laughing like a naughty boy, having walked up unaided and thrown his crutches down the stairs. He did his film and followed this with a play on television which won him the critics' nomination for an Oscar. 'Life begins at 62,' he said. 'It is forbidden to be old.'

At the age of 70 he had an infarct of the heart and was not expected to survive. Five years later, Papa Rietti was still writing, filming, teaching. At 75 he came to stay at my home for one week. He brought with him his violin and a book on a 'new method of fingering'. 'Bobby,' he said to me, 'this system has revolutionized my method of playing the violin,' and he practised eight hours a day, endeavouring to eject a habit of 60 years, and learn an entirely new technique. At the end of the week, he went into hospital for his yearly check up, a tired but inspired man. That same night Papa sent for Mama. He had felt frequent spasms of the heart and did not want to let go her hand. Two hours later, his favourite pendulum clock at home stopped unaccountably. Papa was gone.

I collected a small parcel of his effects from the hospital and I found, scribbled in pencil, a poem Papa had addressed to me that same night.

> *Listen, my son*
> *Listen to my voice.*
> *No ... I am not dead.*
> *I am here by you.*
> *Come close, my son*
> *Do not fear.*
> *It's my soul you hear hovering by*
> *To watch over you.*

During the many years since his death, bus conductors,

dustmen, shopkeepers, fellow artists have stopped me in the street to tell me of the affection they felt for him. His advice, his teaching, his ability and his consideration for the troubles of others, will not easily be forgotten.

What we do here – who we make of ourselves – lives on in people's minds not merely for years, but for centuries. Does not half the world worship a man who was put to death by the Romans 2,000 years ago? Do not the Jews and Moslems pay respect to a man who journeyed from Ur to Canaan perhaps 5,000 years ago to teach mankind there was but one God? Let us not fool ourselves that man ceases with his death. His thoughts, his deeds and his love for his fellows will linger on, to influence others for as long as mankind exists and is blessed with memory.

ᘓ

Farewell, Dearest Mother

F AINTLY – BUT CLEARLY – I heard my mother's emergency bell ring. I dashed from my study and made for her flat adjoining my house, checking on the way that I had not confused the sound with the front-door bell, for it had been so faint, and normally, if she had had to ring for me, it was a harsh, strong sound.

Mother was not in her bedroom; I found her seated in the living-room with the television on. She had felt very poorly and could not muster enough strength to crawl to the other room in order to ring the bell by her bedside. She had tried vainly to call me, and somehow – by means beyond my understanding – this call for help had communicated itself to my ears as the sound of the bell which she had in fact not rung. Once before this had happened; but that time it was my son Jonathan who had clearly heard it and went in to find she had collapsed on the floor due to a stroke – and then too she had been too far from her bell to have reached it.

I gathered her in my arms and carried her to bed. She was very hot and shivering uncontrollably, so I rushed her off to hospital. On examination it appeared she had contracted pneumonia, and I had taken her in just in time. My poor lovely mother was now trembling violently and her jaws chattered so hard, she chipped the edge of a front tooth. She looked close to death's door.

I was sent home and returned early in the morning, to find her sitting up in a long ward, looking rested and ten years younger. She had always displayed incredible fortitude and had more than once recovered from the verge of the beyond. The first time was when she nearly drowned, the second when she was gassed by a faulty geyser in the bathroom, and, more recently – at the age of 78 – when the first of two strokes had paralyzed her entire left side and she lost her speech. By sheer will-power she had regained the use of her limbs and words – only to lose the sight of her left eye in a thrombosis. After specialist treatment, she was told that her eye would remain permanently blind. The optician examined her for bifocal spectacles and said there was no point in making a lens for the dead eye: a plain glass would do.

'No,' said Mother, 'please make a proper bifocal lens for that eye, too. God does strange things sometimes ... and you just never know!' The optician told me he had seldom come across such faith in a patient.

Pneumonia kept her in hospital for ten days. During this time she met another elderly woman in the same ward, whom she recognized as my Hebrew teacher when I was a child. Sarah had been a very active, intelligent woman, who had chaired various committees and raised large sums for many charities in her time. Now, the woman was paralyzed from the waist downwards; unable to communicate more than unintelligible sounds. Nothing could be done for her and she had been kept in hospital for a year because her husband too was now confined to a wheelchair and unable to care for her. He visited her regularly in hospital, when she would weep pitifully, begging to be taken home.

Mother had a way with sick people, and in those ten days, she taught her friend how to enunciate her own name and her husband's, and to say the words, 'Nurse … toilet, please'. When her husband heard his name clearly from her lips for the first time in over a year, he almost fainted and the tears continued to roll down his cheeks. The poor woman had been brushed aside as past help and just left to deteriorate. I'm sure not deliberately, but probably through overwork and sheer lack of time to give her the therapy needed to help her to learn to speak again. As a result of Mother's patience and perseverance, she is now undergoing full therapy and slowly recovering the power to communicate.

When I brought Mother home, she did not lament of those moments close to death, nor of the new misfortune she had suffered. She merely said, 'Now I know why God gave me pneumonia … so that I could help Sarah to speak.'

But none of us can exceed our allotted span, and, finally, after yet another stroke which entirely deprived her of the use of the left side of her body, on the 24th of May, 1979, my mother succumbed, and quietly slipped away to join my father and their Maker.

Hashem has given, Hashem has taken … blessed be the Name of Hashem. May your soul rest in peace, my dearest mother.

ℭℬ

A Gift from Beyond

'YOU'LL HAVE TO make it snappy if you want to finish decorating before the children arrive and fall over that can of paint in the hallway,' said my wife, and I sighed with concern. We were expecting our three teenagers home from Jerusalem for Passover and I had rashly promised to repaint the kitchen in time. I say rashly, but I had no alternative for I simply could not afford a professional decorator.

As I painted the woodwork, I was calculating the cost of the airfares, and the outfits of clothing our youngsters would require immediately on arrival. Both girls would need new high boots, shoes, a couple of dresses and probably underwear; my eldest son was badly in need of a Shabbat suit and new shoes, and he had hinted at wanting a bike! The list seemed endless, and I was concerned about where I was to find the money to pay for it all.

At that moment the front-door bell rang and I went to answer, forgetting that I was dressed in old jeans, torn shirt and overalls – all smothered in paint – and that my image as a well-dressed actor would be destroyed in a flash.

At the door stood a short, plump, middle-aged couple, both smiling in a most friendly manner. The man was the first to speak. 'Mr Rietti? My name is Andrea Manopulous, and this is my wife Katina.' After exchanging greetings, they lapsed into silence – still holding my gaze with that pleasant smile. Feeling somewhat embarrassed, I invited them in, sat them in the entrance hall and apologized for my appearance.

'Mr Robert – forgive the intrusion. You do not know us … but we are familiar with you because your mother told us a lot about you. You see, it was I who bought your mother's house from her when she came to live with you about … yes … it must be a good 16 years ago. She used to visit us afterwards and talked a great deal about you.'

Mr Manopulous continued in the same vein, and I began to wonder what on earth was the purpose of their visit and wish he would come to the point. 'Mr Robert, a few days ago the postman delivered a letter which was really meant for your mother, but I did not realize that until I had slit open the envelope. I am so sorry. Look … here it is.' He handed me an oblong, official-looking commercial envelope and I read the typed address. 'Actually it is addressed to me, not Mother,' I said, and removed the contents. To my amazement, it was notification of a Premium-Bond win and a cheque for £100. I caught my breath as I realized that my mother must have bought the Premium Bond in my name years before without even telling me.

A tear welled up in my eye, for it was as though the spirit of my deceased mother had been aware of my concern about purchasing the children's new clothes, and had sent me a message of comfort from beyond. In my mind's ear I could hear her gentle voice saying to me: 'Don't worry, Bobby … here's a little money to help you. You'll see – everything will be all right.'

I said a silent 'thank you' to my mother and muttered a prayer of praise to Hashem.

Look Up and Dream

When you are disappointed or frustrated ...
Look up and dream, my son.

NO, THAT IS not a quotation from a famous poem, nor pearls of wisdom of the sages: they are the simple words of advice from my father to me when I was an overambitious boy actor, failing my auditions or not getting the parts I longed to play.

My father – may he rest in peace – loved life with a tenacity I can liken only to a mother's devotion to her first-born. To him, each day was a new gift which enabled him to improve on his actions of the day before. He greeted each morning with the same prayer: 'May God grant me more patience than I had yesterday.'

As a boy, I could never understand this, for it seemed to me incompatible with his surge of vitality, his desire to fill the unforgiving minute to the brim, his will to act, to write, to compose, to play the violin, to direct or produce – for he was proficient in all these things.

'How,' I used to ask myself, 'can a man with so many talents and with such a desire to fulfil himself in all of them have the audacity to ask God for patience?' It seemed to me he was praying for the wrong thing. To plead for 36 hours instead of 24 in order to get through the extraordinary programme of work he would set himself each day – this would have made sense to me. But patience? Surely patience meant the ability to wait, and I had no desire to wait for anything. I wanted everything to happen there and then. 'Today' was a vast area in time, a multitude of seconds of which *this* instant was the most imperative.

But in my overeagerness I was unarmed against the worst enemy of any artist: frustration. Oh God, what it was to want to do great things and to be nothing but a forehead pressed against a window. Knowing my impatience, Father would say to me, 'Bobby, you must learn two things: that the first gear is there for a purpose, and that you should accept failures for the lessons they bring. Life is not meant to be easy ... it's meant to be life!'

I began to understand the wisdom of his words only after a succession of setbacks. Only then, when my world seemed to have collapsed and I had no more faith in life, in God or myself, only then did I take Father's advice in the manner he prescribed. I would retire to bed, tell my body to relax – slowly - from my toes to my neck, until my limbs felt like a dead weight and no longer part of me. In that state I found my brain became incredibly clear and I set it a task: to dream that my failure was actually a triumph. My mind conjured up a situation in which I was the hit of the season, the toast of London's theatre-land. Lying there so relaxed I had the strange sensation that my mind actually rose outside my body, and, from a few feet above, looked down in amused detachment at the inert, discarded encasement. It was a feeling of release akin to nothing else I had ever known. Trying to describe it makes me feel foolish and inadequate, but this conscious dreamland I entered refreshed my spirit and gave me renewed vigour and faith in myself. It has served me in great stead many a time since then.

All actors long to reach great heights and few ever do. But as long as we know how to dream success, the fulfilment is less important. It's life and the way we live it which matters most. I have not achieved fame – but I have seen the sun rise over Jerusalem. I may never be a film star – but I have found a partner in life who enriches my very being each day that I know her. I have never played Cyrano, L'Aiglon, Romeo or Hamlet – but I have four beautiful children and 22 grand-children to prove to me there is a tomorrow. These are my realities to keep my corporal self in perspective.

As for the fulfilment of my ambitions, there is always Father's advice to: 'Look up and dream'.

PostScript

If you have any similar stories or experiences that you would like to share (which might be published in a second edition of this book) please write to me care of Vallentine Mitchell publishers.

Robert Rietti